OFF THE RAILS

Off the Rails

MEMOIRS OF A
TRAIN ADDICT

LISA ST AUBIN
DE TERAN

BLOOMSBURY

First published 1989
Copyright © 1989 by Lisa St Aubin de Terán

Bloomsbury Publishing Ltd, 2 Soho Square, London W1V 5DE

British Library Cataloguing in Publication Data

St Aubin de Terán, Lisa
Off the rails: memoirs of a train-addict.
1.   Railroads – Europe – Passenger traffic
2.   Europe – Description and travel – 1971-
I.   Title
385′.22′0924   HE2591.E9

ISBN 0–7475–0011–8

Typeset by Cambrian Typesetters, Frimley, Surrey
and printed in Great Britain by
Butler & Tanner Ltd, Frome, Somerset,

There is no known cure for an obsession with trains. It may strike early in life as was evident in Lisa St Aubin de Terán, infant prodigy of the District Line. Prep school on the railway embankment of East Dulwich Station and the lure of Brighton undoubtedly placed temptation her way, but it was a childhood journey through Russia on the Occident Express that began a lifetime's addiction.

Lisa's first years of marriage were spent largely on trains, slowly criss-crossing the Continent with her dashing husband Jaime and his fellow South American exiles. Withdrawal symptoms were naturally suffered during her years running a sugar plantation in Venezuela – where the very notion of a train is symbolic of all that is wonderful and amusingly unreal.

There were trains, however, to take her through the red dust of Argentina south to Patagonia. And a vast network of trains lay in wait to keep Lisa circulating round Italy and, on regular intervals, to shuttle her to the Norfolk Fens or to Loch Dhu, to romance in Bristol or to marriage proposal from a young stranger on the Düsseldorf Express.

There were trips to Chicago, Ankara and New York City.

The only course of action open to such as Lisa is just to keep taking the trains – to experience and record the shifting scenery of a rich and surprising journey through life.

FOR ALL THE PEOPLE I HAVE MET ON TRAINS

CONTENTS

1

Under the tidemark
with my mother's loves

I would like to say that I was born on the Orient Express as my mother took her bi-monthly trip to Istanbul. Or that I was smuggled out of China as a tiny baby, wrapped in silk and hidden in the guard's van in a trunk of geological specimens. However, I was born in Kensington in 1953, and moved shortly afterwards to Wimbledon, in the days when that was in the county of Surrey and London was a faraway place. My mother had a passion for moving, but she confined it to moving house and changing husbands. So between Kensington and Wimbledon there were actually four more homes which are of little relevance to my tale.

In Wimbledon, where a rusty tricycle and long walks were all that came to vary the humdrum routine of home and watching the girls with pink leotards under grey tunics tiptoe into the ballet school across the road, we shared a fence with the Newby family. Eric Newby was a man who was said to have 'travelled'. In those days, prior to my fourth birthday, I felt that I, too, had travelled, on account of my occasional forays on the 155 bus to such high-spots as Elys, the department store, and the Holy Cross Convent, where my sisters, who were half-sisters, were at school.

On the Eastern Front of our garden, a small crack in a wood knot provided a spy-hole on to the lawns and borders of our other neighbours, and these contrasted so astonishingly with our own ill-kept japonicas and sprawling fruit trees that I used to spend hours staring through this peep-hole into the glamorous world of afternoon teas and island bedding 'over there', in the first foreign country I was to long for. One day, aged three, I suppose, I was less disturbed than the kneeling gardener on the other side of the fence to find myself eyeball

1

to eyeball with someone else. That was the first of many meetings with strangers who became close friends without the benefit – or handicap – of a formal introduction. This particular gentleman, for such he turned out to be, was called Simon, and he introduced the exotic element of snacks on golden plates to my weary, harried mother, and so won the hearts of her four unruly daughters. We were an all-female household, and our china was chipped from many family rows.

There was not enough in the gardens to hold my curiosity for long. Sometimes a man called Morris came to Sunday lunch and then got banished to the shrubbery to chew his way through all the bones of the roast chicken. But even such casual stunts soon palled, and we quickly gave up watching him demolish the carcass.

We lived on the crest of a hill in a suburban haven called Ridgeway Place, and there my sisters, all older than myself, had a gang of friends from which I was permanently excluded. It was this that led to the coupling of the early seeds of my future imagination with a desire for admiration, to bring forth the boastful invention of feats I had never seen, let alone performed. Having seen 'the girls' cycle down the steep hill of our road to stop spectacularly at the main road below, I swam into focus with a tale of riding down this hill while standing on the saddle of my trike, and, without bothering to stop at the junction, crossing straight through the traffic and into a garage on the far side. My fame as a budding stunt rider was short-lived, cut short by a volley of adult complaint. Not until I discovered the Victoria to Brighton line was I to feel such a thrill again.

When I was five, the family's very precarious fortunes collapsed, together with many of the ceilings of Ridgeway Place, and we moved to what was then an insalubrious area of Clapham. If Wimbledon had been a temporary sojourn away from Kensington, and bearable as part of the romantic myth that my mother wove around our family, Clapham was more like a fall from grace. The apple had been bitten, and the fruit turned sour. I don't think my mother ever really recovered from living South of the River. It was somehow too near the bone for her. She herself had grown up in a state of ease salvaged from bankruptcy and looming poverty. It was as though there was a tidemark below which none should go, and we, as a family, had now fallen below it. The row of limes that dropped their sticky, scented flowers on us, as we walked the otherwise drab road to the bomb site and the rebuilt flats that we had moved to, were witness to our shame.

On the far corner of the road, a laburnum tree struggled through the pounded wasteland nominated as a 'garden' to the council estate. This one tree was hacked back as relentlessly as soldiers at Verdun, every shoot and flower mutilated, vandalised – and yet, by some extraordinary power of recuperation, it survived year after year, and flowered. I know that my mother identified with that tree. On another corner of the street there was what was called 'the murderer's house', and this provided years of entertainment and speculation for the local kids. Otherwise, the council flats over the road housed gangs so notorious in the subculture of South London that their very presence was a constant challenge to those of us delinquent and idle enough to brood on them.

My mother still worked in Wimbledon for the first year after our move, together with someone called Commander Stokes, who hated cats, and a man who bred rare German horses. Every day she and I would travel on the Underground's District Line to South Wimbledon, together with a pack of liver sausage or cucumber sandwiches, and a novel for me to read, for after my foray on the tricycle, I had forsworn social intercourse and taken up serious reading. My mother, thwarted in so many ways, warmed to the idea of a super-gifted daughter and encouraged me in my pre-school pursuit of Jane Austen and the Victorians. We would sit on the train, she with her tamed cascade of dark red hair and her copy of *The Times*, and I with my thin pages and small print astonishing the passengers around us. This became such a ritual that I didn't dare disappoint my mother publicly, and relegated *Tin Tin* and *Jo of the Chalet School* and the *Dandy* to secret late-night reads or the lavatory.

The Underground station at Clapham South is a strange, desolate place, approached from the east past the seemingly endless railings of the South London Hospital for Women and Children, and flanked, across the road, by a bunker left over from the last war. The escalator is unnaturally long, a fact that was brought home to me one day when I travelled down it with my mother while Resi, one of my elder sisters, travelled up it on the other side. She was wearing her grey school uniform, and she should have been in her grey school in Westminster. Our eyes met from a great distance, and an instant message of a fate worse than death if I gave her away flashed up to me. It was such a long escalator that I had plenty of time to realise that if our mother saw her, Resi would never believe I hadn't sneaked. It was also so long that I knew that not to see the solitary, grey-uniformed girl on the other side, a person would need to be blind. The escalator crawled; I got cramp and felt sick. Nothing happened, but even now, nearly thirty years later, I still find that particular escalator distressing. It gives me the feeling of time held in suspension and regrouped somehow over my head like a cleaver. It's the 'what if I die here' feeling I get every time I go down into the grey tunnels that guide one on the one hand to 'Bal-ham, the gateway to the South', and towards the river on the other.

1959 was a bad year, so bad that much of its detail has been erased in my head, the better to live with its memory. There were things that touched me immediately – like going to school – and there were things that just ground their heel into the way we lived. It was the year that broke Joanna's back, or, rather, her backbone of resistance.

My mother, up until then, had seen our encampment in darkest Clapham as a very temporary expedient, and one that had saved us, albeit temporarily, from financial ruin. She wrapped her furs and stoles in tissue paper, and put them away in the bottom of her bow-fronted chest of drawers, together with her many packets of love-letters, all bound up in bundles tied with red ribbon. It was a big, deep drawer, and those letters more than half filled it. She had a dream of another world, far away from the grimy monotony of Trouville Road and its dreary parameters, where the poets and artists she had known and loved and lived with in the forties would reign, with their aesthetic values and their generosity. She also had that kind of generosity, and more, because she gave away all that she ever had believing that the same luck that had guided her through the war and the blitz, four marriages and four births, would somehow dredge us all out of our plight.

Our first year in Clapham began to wear everything down. So her beautiful clothes wore shiny in places and frayed, mahogany veneers on tables were scratched, chair legs broke and ornaments were smashed, and as there was no money to replace them the flat gradually shook down to its books and pictures, what was left of the family silver, and a small cabinet of chinoiserie known as the Aunt Connie cabinet. Things were still just all right. Every other Saturday we went to Chelsea to visit my mother's best friend in her smart Georgian house, and while they talked we children played on the giant rocking horse in the nursery while listening to the gossipy laughter below. These visits were often followed by visits to Aunt Mimi, who was a Hungarian clairvoyant and no aunt at all, but who made exquisite flowers out of bread and told stories of gypsies and wolves and suicides in a heavy middle European accent.

Meanwhile, in Wimbledon, Joanna had fallen in love with a New Zealand painter who worked hard all week in the labelling department of Fortnum & Mason. He said that he worked in a basement performing magic. He said he could turn any packet or tin into something wonderful by alchemy. He used to cook rare and to our minds inedible meals with exotic and slimy ingredients. We craved shepherd's pie and tinned fruit salad, but his *haute cuisine* made Joanna smile. Joanna was our mother, whom life was battering, and whatever made her smile made us smile too.

But in 1959 the painter, who was desperately homesick, went away. The plan was that we should all follow, but there was no clear plan as to when. He, after slaving in the basement of Fortnum's for months to get some money together, set off with his friend, Colin, to hitchhike back to New Zealand. It took him well over a year to do it, and during that year Joanna lost her faith in life. Colin, the friend, made the whole trip in a three-piece suit and a bowler hat and spent a large amount of his travelling money on buying the most recent copy he could lay his hands on of *The Times*. We were sent regular and hilarious accounts of their partnership across the seas and deserts of the world. But they were never funny enough to wipe out the hurt and anxiety on Joanna's face, or to block out the sound of her weeping every night into her pillow. No one had ever left her like that; she was too beautiful to leave, and too frail to live without the total love of exceptional men.

And in 1959, I, the infant prodigy of the District Line, after innumerable pâté and cucumber sandwiches, a great deal of swinging round a drainpipe outside the resinous place where my mother worked, and the complete works of Jane Austen, was sent to school. I had moved, as our life grew duller, and more and more bereft of colour and of any chance to escape, in leaps and bounds from novels to the dictionary and Roget's *Thesaurus*. In history and geography I could astound with my grasp of names and dates and places; in botany I had long since outgrown the brilliant rosebay willow herb from the wasteland and could, with the most obnoxious ease, name almost every wayside flower and tree in England, in both English and Latin.

I had then, as I have now, a great need to please the people I liked. I also had then, which I do not, alas, have any more, a photographic memory. This, however, was the year that Piaget's 'playway' took its tightest hold over the previously antiquated primary schools of London. Playing was what children needed to do, and playing was what they had to do in school. I hated playing, and I hated school. My one lifeline was my books, and these were confiscated daily on my way in through the grim entrance marked 'Girls'. The classrooms each had sandpits and water troughs and coloured balls and tambourines, and a lot of chewing gum which had stuck and hardened under everythng. Twice a week, there was a lesson called Musical Movement, which coincided with a programme on the wireless. During this, boys and girls had to stand in their vests and underpants (mine were Harrods best, sadly thin after having been passed down through each of my sisters) and move to the suggestions of the syrupy voice on the set. 'Now I want you to pretend to be an elephant on the moon. You are an elephant, you are not sure where you're going.' I never knew who I was most embarrassed for, myself, or the voice on the radio. 'You are a blancmange struggling to get out of the mould.' I thought about dying, in my threadbare vest, but I felt too young.

Every day, before break and our miniature bottle of milk, we were given a red cod-liver oil capsule. There were dozens of us, dissimilar in many ways but united in one: we all hated cod-liver oil, and we all threw our capsules into a corner of the playground which, over the term, developed a glutinous pink layer and an incredibly fishy smell. I grew to know despair there in the primary school, and to understand more the despair that I witnessed every day at home. And as I learned the grim lesson that dreariness and dullness maim and crush, I managed to gather what energies were left to me and prepare myself for a lifetime of truancy and escape.

I had decided, after one term, that truancy was my only option. Joanna had too many problems of her own for me to feel I could burden her with my own complete inability to adapt to the orchestrated boredom of school. So, instead, I made my appearance there from time to time, always with a forged absence note and an excellent excuse, but most days crept back to our empty flat after everyone had gone. Sometimes I was joined by Resi, who also truanted, but usually I was alone. There I read my way indiscriminately through the many shelves of books and indulged in a great many daydreams. I read Oscar Wilde, and understood very little of it, but certain lines stood out and remained in my head like guidelines to feel my way along on the way out of Clapham and of London itself. He said, 'I never travel without my diary. One should always have something sensational to read on the train.' I had neither diary nor transport, but I began to muster my energies and my dreams in order to discover the means of obtaining, at least, the latter.

My ambition was fed by the visits of my father, arriving at rare and irregular intervals from America, or Mexico, or Paris, or Prague, with taxis and orchids and a life-style entirely different from our own. Whatever bitterness there had been between him and Joanna remained for her, and she spoke to him only reluctantly, preferring not to do so at all.

Everyone called my father Jan (pronounced Yun), and so did I. He used to turn up at anything from three-monthly to three-yearly intervals. I cannot say that his visits were unannounced, as he used to fanfare his arrivals with a deluge of exotic postcards from places all over the world. These would consist of cryptic dates and flight times. I don't think he ever came to see me at one of these prearranged times. Instead, he would telephone to say that a taxi was on the way to take me to our old house in Wimbledon, now his London residence, converted by his neglect into an urban jungle worthy of his voluntary exile from South America.

My pleasure at seeing him easily outweighed the agony of his hugs. Jan is huge and alarmingly charming. His house was like a world embassy, with writers, painters, politicians, presidents-to-be and had-been, actors, models, singers and a host of indescribable others who would gather telepathically on his sporadic visits to town. He was a big man, a term often used by maudlin friends of his. Whenever I was asked what my father did, I would pause, and then lie. It was too hard to explain that he did everything. He was a playwright, novelist, poet, painter, singer, actor, diplomat, politician, journalist, professor and playboy, and extremely successful at all of them.

He was born by the Demerara River in what was then British Guiana, in South America, but he had also lived in New York, London, Paris, Prague, Mexico, Ghana, Cuba and almost anywhere else I ever mentioned. His amorous imbroglios were so numerous as to resemble something out of the Keystone Cops. He seemed to love not only the women but the intrigue as well. His loyalty to me (when present) was such that I was included in his legion infidelities to his lovers,

8

mistresses and wives. My loyalty to him was constantly assailed on these occasions by his vying girlfriends bribing, blackmailing and interrogating me as to his whereabouts, plans and movements. He was taken to be the personification of too many women's dreams of a tall, dark stranger. He was certainly very tall and very dark. When he smiled, an enormous slow-spreading grin, everyone in the world forgave him, except Joanna.

He was best friends with many of his mistresses' husbands, and when passion faded it was the husbands who clung to his charm. When the telephone rang in Clapham, it would, all too often, be a distraught jilted lover desperate to discover whither my feckless father had fled. He travelled continually, as I do, but in his case it was more often for reasons of business and survival. When things got out of hand he used to complain that, because of his size, he couldn't fight with people without maiming them. So he moved on, returning, like a prodigal son, later – always later. He does, after all, have a dose of *mañana mañana* mixed in with his blood.

His family had lived in British Guiana for centuries as pirates, prospectors, mill-owners, farmers, scholars, drunkards and bums. His mother was the proud and formidable Mrs Carew of Almond Street in Georgetown. Descended from Carib Indian queens, she took it upon herself to redress the world's injustice by prayer and vendetta. She carried her frail giant's height like a wrathful angel of mercy, never raising her voice above a whisper while terrorising a small tropical town. Mixed with her Carib blood was German (Hintzen) and Scottish (Campbell), neither of them soft streaks with which to temper her already very moral backbone. Jan's father was a beautiful, gentle man who proved quite unable to stand up to his headstrong wife, turning his face to the wall and dying young in a final act of defiance against her. It was the one successful bid of that handsome Creole – black, Dutch and Portuguese – whose ambition was to be a painter. My grandmama, Mrs Carew, thought painters were socially suspect. She was the matriarch, the gentle dictator whose whole world obeyed her. Jan worshipped his mother. Having been brought up an atheist, I didn't worship anyone. I loved Jan, and was proud of him, but I knew that he had broken my mother's heart and spirit. Had I expected too much of him, he might have broken mine. As it was, I quickly learned to believe neither his postcards nor his many promises, and to make the most of his rumbustious company while he was there.

1960 went the same dull way as 1959, and scared me into believing that I would lead a dull life. Nothing happened for months on end, and the promises of wit and elegance that I read about were in no way reflected in the muddy pond that was the one feature of Clapham Common. Occasionally my sisters and I would paddle in the clear waters of the nearby Agnes Riley Gardens, but these were more ordinary than we cared to admit. We took up many of the local pastimes, like smashing bottles and defacing posters and fighting with the neighbouring gangs. We were branded as snobs, and this often caused fights and slanging matches in the street. It was the colour of our socks that the other kids found unacceptable, since the girls of Clapham wore white socks, while ours were fawn. Looking back, it seems extraordinary that feelings ran as high as they did over this issue, and yet, almost daily, we had to fight our way out of Trouville Road on account of them. I grew to hate my socks. I wanted either to grow a halo or remain invisible. This fighting carried over into the playground, where I had my last and biggest battle with a boy called Lee who was half-Chinese, and thus, I felt, should have known better than to get involved in petty feuds. However, Lee taunted and challenged me one day to such a degree that I leapt on him in the playground and beat him, venting all my frustration on the less visible parts of his body. After some minutes, I started on his head, and left him in a wicked state. I don't think he had half the pent-up rage that I did, and he fought back in a very inadequate way, managing only to hit my face against the tarmac once. We were separated by a member of staff who, unfortunately for Lee, took such things as age and sex into the balance. The next day, a bruised and battered Lee was publicly caned in assembly for his part in the fight. After this, he became my one close friend.

With every day that passed, Joanna grew sicker of our life and lot. She began to pine to such a degree that her boss, the breeder of horses, paid for her to take a cruise on her own. She went to Leningrad, and we children were billeted around the available family and friends. My sisters went to their grandmother in Budleigh Salterton, and I went to stay with old Commander Stokes in his bachelor establishment in Purley. There I lived on a diet of cod's roe on toast, feeling daily sicker, and hoping that I would survive until her return a month later.

Once having left Clapham, I never really saw it again with any true clarity. By an act of will, I blocked it from my world and invented another one so as to endure the otherwise unendurable. Joanna returned, left her job and went to college to qualify as a teacher. We lived off her meagre grant on spaghetti bolognese and pilchard pie, or, when the grant ran out, on a delicacy called tomato potato (rhyming).

For some reason, I believed only a trip to Brighton would cure me of the tummy ache and fever that now filled my days. The pain had been there since Wimbledon, but it had grown through the Clapham months until it reached a dull level of its own that put a glaze over everything. I made more and more frequent visits to the out-patients department of the South London Hospital for Women and Children, waiting, suffused with guilt, on the long wooden benches with Joanna, who was fighting her own battle with depression. The doctors found nothing but the minor glandular disease I had had since I was three, and I became branded as a hypochondriac; worse, I was accused of tormenting Joanna. I learned to live with the pain, and only rarely to mention it, taking twelve aspirin a day and grafting myself on to our dilapidated sofa, where I would watch the seasons change, filtered through the branches of the lime trees outside.

My truancy increased. I devised a way of leaving for school after Joanna had to leave for college, and since I always returned first anyway I took to sleeping, albeit fitfully, from nine until four. That way I could rise at five when she returned and scrape through the evening without anyone realising how ill I'd become.

11

By day, Joanna attended lectures on child psychology and class control; by night, she addressed envelopes for a marketing research firm. Our local doctor, who was a refugee from Czechoslovakia, fought what came to resemble a court case, in its tedious and protracted length, over my need to be in hospital. Month after month he referred me back to the consultant, who in turn rejected me for skiving. I scarcely cared. I had long since forgotten what it felt like to be well, and didn't want a life centred on my lower abdomen; neither did I want to be prodded and probed and picked over at the hospital. On my morbid days I dreamed of dying, and of a kind of universal grief that would accompany the loss of one so brilliant and wasted and wonderful. During my periods of remission from what turned out to be glandular TB, I continued to weave a plan of escape, by train, to Brighton.

Had the primary school of the fishy playground, the broken heads and the fawn socks continued indefinitely, I fear there would be little more to tell of interest and excitement. But at seven I went to the oldest girls' school in London, a school with libraries, and its own botanical gardens, and, last but never least, its own railway bridge leading straight down to a railway embankment and the platform of East Dulwich station.

2

'The days of our youth are the days of our glory'

My first term at James Allen's Girls' School consisted of a series of pleasurable and not so pleasurable shocks. For instance, I discovered that there were lots of clever, literate children in the world, and that several of them were in Lower II. Then, everybody was better at maths than I, and some of them spoke French. On the plus side, however, I had an immensely complicated uniform, bought specially for me and unworn by any sister. I wore this uniform all through the summer before I started at JAGS, as the school was called by those who knew it. I didn't wear it in bed because I wasn't allowed to, but I would have done so had I been able to smuggle it on under my nightdress. The head-bashing stopped, apart from later, more ritualised fights behind the games sheds, and most of the girls disliked the school lunches and were thrilled to find that I could and would eat anything up to a dozen plates full of tepid semolina for them.

For at least six months I determined to learn all I could, both from the school and the (relatively) quiet, well cared-for girls who went there. The hierarchy, rules and jargon were a mystery that took some months to crack. I knew that my only chance of staying on past the preparatory and into the main school was by winning one of the two free scholarships offered each year to the pupils with the best exam results. Lastly, and strangely, as far as I could see not even the seniors played truant.

On those days when Joanna herself deemed me too unwell to go to school, I went with her to her new job in Bethnal Green in the grimy, but never dreary, East End of London. She worked now as a special teacher, not so much teaching as containing problem children. Many of her pupils were delicate, and most of them came from homes where they had been subjected to the most appalling battery and abuse. The 'special school' provided breakfast, lunch and tea as part of a service that tried to compensate for the neglect that was all the children got at home. The scrambled eggs, I remember, came in slabs of yellow jelly and were sliced with a knife. The kids there were more streetwise than any I had ever met, and I learned a great deal from their mistakes, successes and general mastery of the adult world. They taught me, among other things, how to ride the Underground trains for free, how to simulate an epileptic fit and how to spin on my heel while running, thus dodging any pursuers. I never found much use for any of these skills. However, one little boy, Harry, who attended the special school less frequently than the others and whose fair shaved head was misshapen with scars, promised to teach me how to be invisible. Because of the collage of cuts and bruises that Harry always brought with him, I didn't think he'd quite found the secret for himself, but he assured me it could be done. Unfortunately Joanna moved on before he'd had a chance to show me how, this time to a school for the maladjusted, once more in the heart of London's slums. Some of the children here were as delicate as those other problem children, but all of them had been officially branded as not just difficult, but 'bad'. This was the place for inveterate truanters, and for arsonists and shoplifters, for bullies and head-bashers.

The school seemed to be run along Dickensian lines, with tiny cupboards to lock unruly pupils in and a lot of beatings and pulling of children's hair and twisting of ears and arms by certain members of the staff. One, in particular, used to control his class by keeping a sash window open and then making a kid lean out while he crashed the window down on the back of a neck or back. The children all seemed used to this sort of treatment, and since the next stop was a long-term, live-in reformatory, they seemed to accept it philo-sophically. Joanna suffered in that job, struggling both to earn her living and to change the system. She had started there on a temporary assignment and was due to move on after three weeks. When the time came for her to leave, she couldn't bring herself to abandon her class, choosing instead to stay with them for several years. Her class quickly came to adore her.

My childhood was dogged by delinquent children, and, later, adolescents with crushes on my mother. They used to follow her home, and wait for her when she went shopping. Weekends and holidays were always peppered with their problems. Joanna loved and treasured lame ducks, seeming to carry, wherever she went, an imaginary shrimping net in which to gather other people's sadness. It was as though it in some way obliterated her own.

No two schools could have been more different than the barrack-like, defaced viciousness of my mother's and the tranquil beauty of the grounds and gardens where I studied. One day I would sit in a class of well groomed, over-fed girls, the immaculate daughters of the well-to-do; the next, I would be in the back row of a classful of tattered, scabby urchins. At home there was a growing library of books on delinquent children, and these I waded through, but could find little to compare in their theories with the reality of the sash window crashing down like a blunt guillotine. And none of it did anything to change my desire to move on.

Much of those six months I spent trying to be like the other girls, at least superficially, and to disguise what I really was. Unlike Joanna, I wasn't actually ashamed of my upbringing, and I had no true concept of what it meant to be 'South of the River', but I did quickly grasp that her four marriages and our atheism, my dozens of eccentric step-relations, Joanna's bohemian past and my father's bohemian present, were non-subjects at school, since they caused shock reactions of a seemingly viral nature that could linger and rebound. The temptation to embroider the potential scandal of home was resisted and a semblance of normality main-tained by a network of white lies. Perhaps because of my many truancies, or because of some congenital disability, or perhaps because of my laziness, I never got past my first phys-ics lesson, and even that one class was never fully understood.

When we went shopping in Abbeville Road, the one trading street in the neighbourhood, the whispers, silences and stares were never far away and the gossip that was growing around our unorthodox household followed us from shop to shop. Abbeville Road was like a trench that was constantly filling with water, and the shopkeepers had the forlorn air of those about to go under. It was a long street, and it had an extraordinarily depressing effect on me as I walked down it, watching the drowning faces through grimy windows or behind the shop counters. Only Joanna treated Abbeville Road as though it were the food hall of Harrods, ordering impossibly esoteric goods in minute quantities. These, though not only unobtainable but actually unheard of, she would continue to demand, beginning the purchase that would end in a sachet of coffee crossing the counter with a request for a quarter of a pound of Costa Rican high roast, medium ground, please, and very fresh, and before settling for a sweating wedge of Cheddar launching into her usual reel of Saint Paulin, Brie and Dôme Blanc. When Joanna didn't go shopping herself, she sent us, her daughters, to shop for her, and my embarrassment at having to return and return again to complain either of the quality or of the quantity of the anyway shoddy products was overwhelming. So the snide remarks and the gossip grew. And we girls combated them by spreading outrageous rumours and concocting weird stories that would really give them something to talk about.

Sometimes we would stage fights in our flat. The best of these would be when Lali and Resi's father, Andrew, came to visit. A lot of people would see him go in, and then report his presence there, thus arousing the local interest. With a couple of wet tea towels, we would slap the walls and furniture in the sitting room, while Lali and I would whine and call out for mercy, and Andrew would shout and threaten to kill us. This performance, when it didn't end in hopeless giggling, wound up with a prolonged bout of simulated weeping and sniffing. Because of the thin walls of the flats, it would be quite audible not only to several sets of neighbours, but also from the street. I think the neighbours tired of our games long before we did as a family. When it became clear that we were not going to move away in the foreseeable future, the battle lines relaxed a little and we settled into a routine of carving hangmen in the wet cement and breaking bottles, knocking on people's doors, and planning journeys to places where the name of Clapham would ring no bells.

I first discovered trains as a means of truancy, and thus they have remained, irrevocably linked in my mind with the idea of escape. They are the vehicles of romance and adventure, a lifeline promising relief from dullness. I have woven a network of fantasy around the very concept of the train, so wide that the actuality of the journey can rarely outweigh the overall sense of glamour and daring which rail-travel has in my head. Myths begin naturally and then are moulded and sculptured and treasured until they grow out of all proportion to the initial grain of truth. My own love of the railways hovers now somewhere between the improbable and the insane. Sometimes, as I squeeze my way through grime and empty beer cans, past over-stressed commuters or over-wrought shoppers or over-sexed hikers, and the trains are late and the loos blocked and the buffet closed, I stand in wonder at the lengths to which I will go to foster my dream. This dream is of travel and romance, and of romantic travel. I have spent years in seemingly purposeless drifting, but I believe that when I search it is for a moment when time stands still – the pause in the ballet leap, the volatile thrill of perfection. Travelling is like flirting with life. It's like saying, 'I would stay and love you, but I have to go; this is my station.' For the rootless and the restless, and the just plain curious, it is a way of being inside the kaleidoscope, but with a way out and a flexible timetable.

Many a one before me has stirred to great railway journeys. But when I say I love trains, I mean I love them all. Not just the wild and wonderful ones, but the ones that go from Liverpool Street to King's Lynn and Colchester, and the ones from Paddington to Bristol Temple Meads, the night trains and the day trains and even the little shuttles from Waterloo to Kingston-upon-Thames and others of that ilk. Brighton was my first dream to come true, and the train journey there my first taste of this recurring magic.

Before I ever went to Brighton, I loved it. Regency bucks went there, and the Prince Regent lived there, and, more recently, people from all over England went there for dirty weekends. I pictured the sea crashing (with a rather northerly force) against the pier, and I envisaged palm trees lining the sand. My mother came from Jersey, where, allegedly, there were palm trees, and my father came from South America, where there were definitely palm trees, and I felt it was my birthright to frequent the places of this world where palm trees grew and the sea crashed restlessly against the shore. Harriette Wilson, my heroine, had lived in Brighton, and her famous memoirs began there with the intriguing sentence, 'I shall not say why and how I became, at the age of fifteen, the mistress of the Earl of Craven.' She continues, 'I resided on the Marine Parade, at Brighton; and I remember that Lord Craven used to draw cocoa trees, and his fellows, as he called them, on the best vellum paper, for my amusement.' I felt a great desire to 'go the whole way' (hence my fascination with the concept of the dirty weekend), and Brighton, at the end of the line, beyond which no train could go without tipping into the sea, represented for me the perfect truancy.

The journey through the suburbs was like a slow escape route taking me away from all that I disliked and feared to be contagious towards all that I loved and hoped to be fired by. The litany of grey places remains stamped on my mind, from Clapham Junction with its seething jumble of tracks strewn over a dead zone of gasworks and scrap metal and blackened bricks to the first glimpse of the sea itself: Wandsworth Common, back gardens and tacked-on bath-rooms; Balham, slipped slates huddled in grime; Streatham Common, spiked railings edged in blackberries; Norbury, tidy patios in place of the more southerly junk. Each side of the track is lined with black spikes, iron railings to impale the traitors on. So on and on to Thornton Heath, Selhurst, and East Croydon and South Croydon appearing like a suburban stutter anxiously repeating all the stations before.

Purley was always the first touchstone of freedom. Purley had coalheaps and a miniature railway in the air to transport the coal. Having stayed in Purley with Commander Stokes, I knew every inch of his booby-trapped back garden, with its magnolia stellata and its owner's war on cats: all cats, to the death and without quarter. I remembered his weaponry, and also the station. The wild daisies crept in in Purley, and the iron spikes disappeared, and the countryside began. Now there were no more grimy parks or half-hidden trees, but little cliffs or chalky shrubs stretching up from the window to the sky.

At Eastwood there was a great country house with red and white towers, and a park. Then the need to be near the sea took over, a sense of its smell, a longing to glimpse its grey waves, and walk on its pebbly shore, and throw stones until my shoulders ached, and then to wander through the Metropol, brushing past its potted palms and pretending to myself not that I stayed there but that I lived there by the sea and always would. 'Always' being until such time as I moved on in my fantasy, which would be about three o'clock. Time to cover the grey track in reverse. Time to get home from 'school'. Time not to be missed.

After discovering my means of escape to Brighton, just over an hour away – one hour to freedom – I never hated Clapham again in quite the same way. I realised, after my first visit, that the palm trees on the beach were not to be, but unlike the notorious and ambitious Harriette Wilson, who regularly fell asleep over Lord Craven's bedtime lectures on cocoa trees when she lived with him in Brighton, and felt, on leaving him, or rather on being left by him, that her heart was 'the lighter for my release from the cocoa trees', I never grew tired either of the place itself or of my illusion of its palms. I soon realised that a grand hotel is the safest place for a small child to wander unaccompanied and not raise suspicion, and although the palms at the Metropol were potted, they were still vaguely tropical and a lot better than the platoons of dusty aspidistras that darkened the windows of many a tea room in the humbler parts of town.

I became a reformed character, setting off to school with zeal each morning. All the boredom of the previous years was banished; now I had real goals to achieve, plans to fulfil, places to go. Having been caught once, at the infant school, for truanting, I was determined not to be caught again, partly as a point of personal pride, but mostly to avoid distressing Joanna, who believed in my virtues with such passion that, had she been pope, I could have been canonised. In making the choice to specialise in problem children, she may have been surprised to discover she excelled in her specialisation to the point of producing several of her own. I, however, was not supposed to be one of them. I was the goody-goody, the gifted, tragic child too wise for this world, whose sweetness cloyed all over Clapham and its environs. I loved my sisters, and, more surprising, they loved me. Given my position as Joanna's favourite, I wouldn't have blamed them had they shunned and hated me. Instead, while Gillie studied, Resi, Lali and I combined our criminality. I shared the benefits of my safe conduct pass at home, and we were so close that no outside force could divide us.

Brighton was bigger than that, though. I never shared Brighton at home. It seemed too adventurous and too bizarre. To go there once, say, for a dare, would have been all right, but to travel there regularly would have seemed too weird. Resi would have worried not for my safety but my sanity, and Lali would have just worried. I began to study, not, like my peers, for the eleven plus examination, but for a fool-proof strategy that would get me to the seaside and back time and again and yet allow me to be in the right with absolutely everybody.

Joanna used to visit a lady whose daughter had a serious kidney disease, and I would go with her sometimes, and sit and listen to the daily worsening of the girl's symptoms and her struggle with the treatment. The girl in question had an ethereal look about her, and this made me notice my own rather unearthly appearance – the pallor, the dark-ringed eyes, the thinness of the face, the feverish flush, all marking my as yet undiagnosed TB. When I travelled on the Brighton line, I found that the simple invention of a similar kidney condition for myself and a constant need to shuffle between imaginary (but named) doctors in both London and Brighton, provided me with a great many middle-aged, well-to-do businessmen dipping their hands in their wallets for my child's tickets on that line. I used to tell a tale of woe, explaining how my own ticket had come to be lost. I found that by sitting very still and reading a good book, and looking really sad, someone would always approach me first and either ask me what was up or tell me that it might never happen. As the months wore on, I acquired a guardian aunt in Brighton and a sick mother in London, and the names of hospitals, streets and drugs to round out my story. I wore my school uniform, with certain inspired loans from my sisters' uniforms, so as to look neat and respectable, but not identifiable.

I cannot vouch for the saying that 'If one tells the truth one is sure, sooner or later, to be found out.' But I know that if one does not tell the truth often enough, the lies somehow become fact. Thus the ticket collectors and the guards at either end of my route knew me by sight and name and greeted me each time our paths crossed. They knew me as Lizzie, and they all knew jigsaw pieces of my story and my imaginary disease. I was a brave little soldier struggling to survive, as one of the guards used to put it. At nine I claimed to be a stunted twelve year old, and by the time I was really twelve I was already an established part of their routine and nearly grown up for them to boot.

Looking back, I suppose I was incredibly lucky to have made so many trips and never once be bothered by a pervert. I should add, lucky in those days, because, subsequently, perverts seem to have crawled out of the woodwork to flock around me as I travel. But in my childhood I remained unmolested and unaware of any kind of sexual advance, despite frequent and often long conversations with solitary middle-aged men. Maybe my illness kept them at bay, I don't know. Later, at least, when the staff of that part of the south-eastern railways grew used to me, I felt protected by their concern.

On the days when I travelled to school, I did so on the top of a number 37 bus, which I used to catch on the edge of Clapham Common at a stop known as 'The Pavement'. This bus-stop was the usual sort of affair but pincered between an

outsize clothes shop and a hosier's that sold some extraordinarily outmoded camiknickers which it displayed in its
window for many years until the weak sun faded them.
Opposite the stop was a raised bunker from the war grassed
over and planted with about three crocuses and a daffodil. At
one end there was a stone drinking trough for horses, and at
the other a mock-Tudor clock tower presiding over the
entrance to the tube station. Dulwich was not accessible by
tube, so only the 37, or at a pinch a 35-and-change, could
guide me through the streets of Lambeth to the high,
wrought-iron gates of my school. Brixton, the scene of many
future riots and ghetto violence, had not yet emerged from its
chrysalis of terminally faded gentility. There was a grey
apathy like a layer of dusty mould over everything there,
brightened only by a magnolia tree outside the dilapidated
public library. This magnolia used to blossom with amazing
profusion every spring.

Sometimes the slow double-decker bus would stop at a
place called Herne Hill, and at other times I would just
choose to stop there. On these occasions, I'd take an
overground train to East Dulwich Grove and arrive with the
many girls who commuted daily from Kent. From the
platform one could look up and see the wide bridge that
linked the school gardens to the playing fields, just as from
the bridge one could look down and see the railway-lines
leading into and out of the station. Outside the biology lab
lay part of the botanical gardens, and beyond these was a
reconstructed country lane. It was here that we used to go for
our nature walks, gathering leaves and seeds and burrs to
stick in our scrapbooks, and it was here that I first noticed
how the wild hedgerow thickened into a mass of shrubs and
brambles throttled by bindweed and old man's beard. At one
point, almost concealed, there was a gap in the thicket hedge.
When I was new to the school and wishing to please my new
teacher, I had half scrambled through this gap the better to
reach an abandoned bird's nest on the far side of it. My
teacher called out, 'Lisa, don't go through there, dear, it's
very dangerous, you might fall down on to the railway
track.'

Neo-Holmsean deduction led me to see that this was the one point where one might actually fall on to the platform. The gap had clearly been formed by other users, but in all my years of climbing through it, which ranged from trips to Brighton to quick journeys home or even just a sprint to the kiosk by the station to buy iced lollies and take them back to hot summer sessions of games, I never saw anyone else using it.

The trains themselves were all divided into small compartments unlinked by any corridor. This both provided a great deal of privacy and lumbered one with inescapable travelling companions. Whereas when I travelled to the south coast I never had any problems with other passengers, I often found myself importuned during the seven minutes that I covered to East Dulwich Station. Sometimes this would be by children from local schools who hated all the girls from JAGS on principle. As soon as we put our hats on, we were snobs and they were plebs and only abuse was allowed to pass between us. Some of us younger girls tried to avoid these confrontations by carrying our hats on to the train, but to no avail. The other kids could spot a JAGS hat under four layers of camouflage. Sometimes the intruders would be girls I couldn't bear from school, usually higher up, or prefects. And once it was a madman. My first ever madman. He used to choose my narrow cabin on the train and come and sit opposite me and stare. He was not, by any means, the first man to stare at me, so I thought little of his company until it became persistent. When I sat alone on a train, I could talk to my imaginary companions, but when anyone was actually there I would feel too shy to talk at all. Thus his presence inhibited me, and gradually I began to notice him, sad-eyed and silent, watching me from the far corner. There was a tunnel just before the station, and each time we plunged into its darkness, my madman moved a little closer along his tartan seat.

I felt that he was waiting for me sometimes on the platform at Herne Hill. I didn't always go to school, and I didn't always take the train when he did, so his waiting must have been frustrating in its uncertainty. Weeks went by, and this man neither spoke nor flashed nor did anything improper, he just stared, until, one day, the train stopped between stations and waited for over ten minutes, delayed for some reason of its own. Then the man stood up, still in his corner, and whispered, 'I love you, I love you,' over and over again. I flushed with pride. He wasn't much of a looker, but he was a man, and I was nine, and no one had ever said this to me before, despite my having read the words so many times in novels. I was so taken by it all that I scarcely noticed the train moving again, or the man (my admirer) opening the carriage door. It was only when I felt the gush of freezing January air that I realised the door was swinging free and the train in motion, and the madman standing, rocking by the open door, saying, 'Come and jump with me, because I love you.' He did a few more semi-lurches, and said a few more come on, jump and it'll all be over quicklies, then East Dulwich slid into view, and the train stopped and I dashed out past him, blushing all the way along the platform and up the wide steps and into the street. That night I went home by bus.

3

The Cold War: from London to Leningrad

I didn't know it then, but that one madman set a pattern for much of my life – inspiring sudden loves in strangers and then running away.

At eight, I achieved my childhood ambition and went to Brighton. At nine, from having never been further abroad than Land's End, I was to travel all the way to Leningrad, where my cups of tea at the Metropol on the seafront were transformed into three months of touring Russia's grand hotels. I may have been born with delusions of grandeur; what Russia did was make them real.

It was to be the first and last time I would ever spend with my parents together, since they had virtually not been on speaking terms from the time I was born, and they never would be again. That summer, however, we set off, mother, father and daughter, in an ancient Daimler to drive across Europe, from London to Leningrad. We were going at the invitation of the Soviet Writers' Union, and we were going to spend my father's accumulated and very substantial royalties there, it being then, as I believe it still is, impossible to bring any money out from behind the Iron Curtain.

The trip was made in the spirit of a family *glasnost*, but as the car veered across the roads, missing hedges and ditches as the arguing continued, I began to worry about how we were to return home if the disagreements got out of hand. Joanna kept threatening to get out of the car if my father continued to drive at over ninety miles an hour. He kept explaining, over and over, that there was some fault in the steering that made the whole car shudder, and that the only way to stop this was to travel at high speed. When the Daimler didn't shudder, it raced, and when it wasn't racing, it was shuddering. By the time we left Holland the atmosphere was decidedly strained, even through the glass panel that separated me and the cocktail cabinet from my parents. Through West Germany, recriminations were rife. By East Germany, the bitterness was silent, but no less real. In Warsaw, a truce was called. Poland, at that time, was cobbled throughout, and the wrangle about the internal antics of the car was drowned in the endless jolting and bumping.

Joanna often complained, in later years, that on the outward journey I did nothing but read a book called *Jenny* by Paul Gallico, to the exclusion of all else, including the scenery. 'Every time I looked back,' she accused me, 'you'd be reading that damned book.' And it was true. It is a good book, and one I greatly enjoyed. It was also the only book (apart from Byron's *Don Juan*) I had with me. Most of the actual words being hurled about in the front of the car were lost to me, thanks to the sliding glass window, designed in grander times for privacy. However, the gist of it was not, and I felt a cowardly compulsion to ignore the whole affray in the hope that it would just go away. To influence, or even comprehend, my father's behaviour would have been like trying to plough the sea. My father was six foot six, and my mother was five foot eleven. I, as I informed my conscience, was only nine, and still convalescing from months in bed with grumbling TB.

Joanna was map-reading, not a happy choice. Despite having spent the years of her adolescence in a German convent in London, where she learned how to give the Nazi salute with a hockey stick, it seemed she really did think life was too short to learn the language. Thus we took what she swore was a short cut to Frankfurt, but what actually turned out to be a top security military route, deep into a military zone. As we sailed down the completely empty road, scarcely noticing the grim rolls of barbed wire that fenced it, Joanna was gloating over having escaped all the previous traffic. The barbed wire, which had, until then, confined itself to the sides of the road, loomed up suddenly and completely blocked the way. Further back, some two or three miles, there had been a long metal bridge. After some brief and unflattering discussion concerning my mother's powers of orientation, and during which I studied *Jenny* hard, we turned round. The signs at the approach to this bridge were in German, and they seemed to consist mostly of a lot of *achtung*s and *verboten*s. These were freely interpreted as indicating we were on the road to Frankfurt. There was a gathering of people at the other end. As we drove across, these people started running towards us. A shot was fired, and we stopped. The car was surrounded by grey soldiers banging on the windows and waving their guns. We got out, only to be pushed and poked by rifle butts and angry fists. Joanna met the stream of invective that greeted our descent with the few phrases that she seemed to know. I didn't speak any German, but it didn't take much to understand that we were in a military zone and could be shot. We were shoved along the rest of the bridge on foot and taken to a wooden sentry post. By this time we had all grasped where we were and what the chaps were saying. Joanna's reaction was to gabble nervously, coming out with the German equivalent of things like, 'I see the herons are nesting on the church again this year.' Because she kept repeating this, I think the officer in charge suspected us of spying and trying to get a password across. After a while, even he realised that he was just dealing with tourists who had somehow strayed into this supposedly heavily guarded zone. But he was a man, not unique in this world, who hated the English. The only thing, I think, that saved us, was my father's obviously foreign appearance and the German car, which was searched thoroughly and then confiscated for two hours. The shouting continued, and Joanna, who hates shouting, started crying. This seemed to be the only way our guard could tolerate an English woman, because he became fractionally more conciliatory after that. My father urged me to weep as well, and I did.

We returned, chastened, to the Autobahn, and from there we rattled into Poland. All the way to Warsaw the car survived on a mixture of low octane petrol, diesel and mud.

In German, when a soldier tells you you're dead, at least the general idea gets through. In Polish, the language of few vowels and many consonants of the ż, ć and w variety, no meaning whatsoever permeates into the English mind. For two days we wandered around the towns and villages of southern Poland looking for food. The shops seemed to have a way of selling by producing things wrapped in thick, grainy brown paper from under the counter. In Poznań, we located a restaurant and made an eager study of the Polish menu. We chose three things, by pointing at three different words, made up of different combinations of z's, c's and w's from three different places on the card. Forty-five minutes later we were served three bowls of unsweetened junket. Further along our route, we discovered another tiny restaurant. This one had no menu. In elaborate sign language we ordered a bit of everything, but again we were served small bowls of tepid, semi-solid, unsweetened custard.

We stayed in Warsaw for a couple of days to sate our hunger and to repair the car. On our way out we bought several bottles of strawberry juice, some ham and a huge loaf of black bread which I was delegated to grab from under the counter of a big shop and then pay for. The ham was delicious and lasted about five minutes; the strawberry juice was divine; but the bread was so hard that none of us managed to break into it. It was too large to bite, it broke one of our knives and bent another, nor could rocks smash it, so it stayed with us until we reached the Russian steppes, when it was finally jettisoned from the car window.

Wherever we stopped, a crowd of people would gather around the car and stroke its still-gleaming silver paint, while greeting our attempts to find things to eat not with derision, but with hilarity; this act was admired in many small villages along the way, like a travelling circus. In contrast, from Brest-Litovsk to Leningrad, we were plied with hospitality, pulled and cajoled into people's rooms and cabins to share their food and drink. At an inn near Minsk we dined with a delegation of strangers who talked at us for hours over jugs of kvass. Our trip had already proved to be a tour of some of the most squalid lavatories imaginable, most of them consisting of a hole in the ground. The hole was all well and good; it was what was around it that graded them from the merely insanitary to the grotesque. The inn had an infinitely more hygienic system: a great stream of the nearby river had been diverted to flow under a wooden bench with a hole in it. As I entered the dim shed, I could hear the water rushing under my feet. I sat down over the hole, and very nearly fell in. It was a long drop down, and I was hanging for some seconds by my knees and hands before I managed to drag myself back into the room.

We reached Leningrad on the ninth day after leaving London. Joanna and I shared a suite at the Oktober Hotel, the roubles flowed and I tasted a degree of luxury I had never known before, but would always hanker after in the future. Old Leningrad was so beautiful I could scarcely take it in. I stood in wonder before the Winter Palace one day, only to find it outstripped by the miraculous Summer Palace on its island on the gulf of Finland: Peterhof, with the water gardens and the cascading steps. My father had, by this time, returned to Moscow, leaving us entirely in the hands of our guide, who took us over the hundreds of bridges that link the many islands that make up Leningrad. She was a lovely woman, who as a child had lived through the siege of Stalingrad, as Leningrad was then, and whose entire family had starved there before it was over. Before we left, she gave me her one heirloom, a tiny, hand-painted Russian box which she had salvaged from the wreckage of the devastated city. She said it had been passed from mother to daughter for generations, and that her own mother had given it to her just before she died during the siege. Then she explained that as she had no daughter of her own, and never would have, she had been looking out for years for someone to hand it on to, and had decided that it should be me. I have treasured it ever since, and it is one of the two possessions I have that go with me whenever I travel.

From Leningrad we went to Moscow, where the two best things for me were the Underground and the zoo. The Underground was vast and cavernous, more like a great museum than a tube station, a museum studded with little booths where men could spray themselves with heady scent for a modest price and everyone else could share in an aromatic gassing on the train. Joanna particularly loathed

29

the London Underground, which she always found too crowded and too sordid to bear. I suppose the squalor of the back streets of South London and the East End were more than enough for her without wading through litter and grime on her way between the two. So when we discovered the spotless, polished, inlayed mosaics and paintings of the Moscow Underground, she was as happy as I to travel up and down it merely for the sake of the décor.

We ended our stay at a resort called Sochi by the Black Sea, spent the remainder of our time sunbathing on beaches and making friends. My father came to visit us there with a gang of young Georgians who had been crammed into his car for days and were testing the endurance of his liver by giving him enormous quantities of vodka to drink. He looked very yellow, but seemed, as always, to be enjoying himself. For breakfast we were encouraged to eat porridge bowls full of red caviare and pints of yoghurt, but I was more of a frankfurter and cheese person. Then he was gone again, and I was left to my own devices with a tow-haired boy called Vovo who promised to marry me some day, while Joanna basked in a circle of admirers further along the beach. Vovo taught me to speak Russian and to back-flip off the concrete wall that divided the shallow water from the submarine depths beyond.

We'd travelled out to Russia a family, luxuriously if bad-temperedly ensconced in the Daimler. Joanna and I returned, long before the Black Sea summer ended, alone, by train. It had not been possible to spend all our roubles, since everything was so cheap and there were so many, so we boarded the Occident Express at Leningrad ready for one last blow-out in the dining car, before crossing the Iron Curtain to re-enter the world of pilchard pies and endless lengths of spaghetti.

It was a beautiful train. Every accessory was polished and glinting. We had a lot of luggage, but even Joanna's, which always seemed to have a life of its own, starting a journey neatly packed into a single suitcase but expanding within days to fill trails of carrier bags, was as nothing compared with the bundles and bags that all the other passengers were carrying. The station was packed with people from all over Russia, and they surged and swarmed along the different platforms not only to catch their own trains but also to look into others. We boarded, and found our compartment without any difficulty since we were travelling, thanks to our roubles, first class. The rest of the train disappeared out of sight, graduating from first to second to third and on into a sort of cattle-wagon-style fourth class.

Our cabin was upholstered in blue, and was large enough to walk about in if one wasn't too ambitious. It reminded me of Queen Victoria's favourite coach from the transport museum in Clapham. At the end of the first-class corridor, a little shrivelled man in a pristine uniform sat huddled in an alcove over a samovar of tea. He offered me a cup, which I took, nursing it back to the blue haven of my room. Outside, on the platform, people were still struggling with enormous string bags stuffed with watermelons and loaves of bread. Inside, beyond the huddled guard, was a first-class dining car already laid with starched white cloths and gilded china, fresh flowers and champagne buckets. The tea was good, sweetened with black cherry jam, a custom I had grown to like. Joanna went off to inspect the rest of the train, leaving me on a half-size upholstered chair in a reverie of blue satin, my delusions of grandeur dangerously inflated. Every few minutes, heavily laden, noisy passengers from the rest of the train would burst in on my cabin and grunt appreciatively. From time to time, the shrunken guard would chide them away, but on the whole he was content to let them be. Joanna, however, was less tolerant, and on her return shooed them away and locked our door from the inside. Across the platforms other trains were lined up, ready to travel down the arteries of Europe and Asia Minor for destinations as far-flung as Siberia and Samarkand.

Somehow, the bickering and the familiarity of the Daimler had filtered the novelty of the lands I had travelled through on our outward journey. Now, watching the coloured silks and embroided caps, the waistcoats and boots and wraps and watermelons, I felt swept up on an exotic wave, the crest

31

of which I was to ride for many years to come. Moscow Central is marked in my memory as a coming of age, forcing open, like a glove stretcher, the passages of my brain to encompass a new geography. My fifty-minute rides to Brighton faded into insignificance. Orpington and Ashford could never be as exciting again.

It was dark when the whistles started blowing for our train, and there was a great deal of last-minute banging on windows as we pulled out of Moscow. Joanna and I changed for dinner that night. I wore a sort of turquoise-skirted ball dress that I had inherited from one of my sisters, and although I felt a princess in it I see from an old photograph that it made me look rather a twit.

Only four other people were travelling first class. They were Russians, and they nodded as we passed them in the dining car. I took one of the flowers from the vase on the table to add to my collection. I had flowers from Pushkin's tomb (asters), from Tolstoy's garden, from Peterhof and, of course, from Vovo, my betrothed. (At Dover, later, I was to notice with horror that flowers were not allowed in, but since I had been collecting them for three months I smuggled them through Customs anyway. Ever since, when I pass through a Customs hall, I feel the same fear that I felt then, smuggling my pathetic living plants into England, expecting to be pounced on at any moment and run through with a bayonet.) The flowers were lovely, but by morning I was to wish I had taken from the table some bread and the extra cheese, and anything else that was edible, instead. The food was good, not exquisite, perhaps, but good, and more than enough.

Then came my first night of train sleep. There is nothing so comforting as a deep sleep on a train. Even a lover will only rock you for so long, but the rhythm of a train in motion is continual, and the most soothing, lulling movement in the world.

Very early the next morning I was awakened by the sound of shunting and clanging. The sun had newly risen, and there were grey guards outside our train, which was stationary at the frontier post of Brest-Litovsk. Joanna had remembered, half-way through dinner, that in three days' time she would be back in London administering to the maladjusted, and the thought was slowly poisoning her journey home. So she didn't share my enthusiasm for the bright daylight that I was letting in to our compartment through the lifted blind, nor did she care for the noisy activities outside our window. After a while we played Bezique. I tried to cheer Joanna up, little knowing that on our return it would be I that would sink with peritonitis and the perennial TB, and spend a year in the South London Hospital in and out of the operating theatre and the intensive care ward. Soon, the first-class guard brought us two cups of Russian tea, which we drank gratefully. This time he asked to be paid.

'Dollars will do,' he volunteered.

He had probably seen far more dollars than we had, since they weren't much in demand in Clapham. I had a pound, sterling, which I gave him. He smiled graciously, and made to retire. I felt too embarrassed to ask for change, but Joanna had eaten too many pilchards not to, so she insisted and was grudgingly given a handful of kopeks.

I watched the sun rise in the sky. Nothing happened. On an adjoining platform, a restaurant car was standing on its own. Between washing and dressing and waiting, and more Bezique, we remarked on its similarity to ours. No breakfast came, and the door to our dining car was firmly locked. After several hours the train was inspected. Then our passports were inspected by a handsome young guard who seemed very taken with Joanna and spun out his duties with a great deal of flattery and flirtation in English that was halting but very attentive to verb tenses. Finally he said he had to go, and left our cabin, taking with him all our foreign and Russian currency, which he replaced with a set of utterly useless traveller's cheques which he swore to be valid the world over.

He had passed from praising Joanna's hair to listing the countries in which these Soviet cheques would be welcome with scarcely any alteration in his tone.

'You are having lovely hair. I am liking lovely hair. I was having liked Russian hair, but now I will be liking your hair . . .

33

'I was thinking your hair is being lovely. You know, you are also having lovely eyes. I am liking lovely eyes,' etc. Had he been fractionally more honest, he might have said, 'You are having lovely cash, I am liking lovely cash,' but, instead, he merely eulogised on the love that other countries felt for the bits of paper that he gave us.

There was nothing we could do, although Joanna gave him the sort of telling off that she probably gave small boys at her school when they spat or swore or peed in the aspidistra.

After this we played Bezique again, sending the mindless brass-tipped markers round their score cards again and again. Slowly, we left the station, Joanna's young admirer blowing her a kiss from the wooden shed where he was smoking with his colleagues. Joanna gave him an unspoken Italian *addio*, with two fingers.

I don't know exactly when we realised that the dining car on the platform was in fact our dining car, and that there was to be no more food until Holland. The quaint peasants with their string bags of melons and chickens and loaves of bread had all come prepared; only we, it seemed, didn't know that it was picnic or starve. I realised now that when the man with the samovar had said, 'What difference can it make? You won't have it soon anyway,' about the pound and the change, he'd been referring to the mustachioed bandits at the frontier, and not to our annual rate of expenditure. He might just as well have kept any number of pounds, and now we wished he had, since he was our only hope and he was not pleased with us. I told him we regretted asking for change, and he shrugged. He'd lived through the war and Stalin and God knows what else, so he wasn't much impressed. You can't eat apologies. They don't buy socks.

Over the next twenty-four hours, Joanna and I both became greedy for his bitter tea, and I began to barter for it, producing gloves, bras and even a suspender belt from our luggage in return for the small glasses he filled from his samovar.

Every time I set off down the corridor to visit him in his little curtained cupboard, he pretended not to know what I'd come for. My conversations on the beach at Sochi with the bronzed and proposing Vovo had taught me enough Russian to carry on fairly fluent conversations. Stretched out on the sand, planning our future lives with very scant regard for such obstacles as the Iron Curtain or the cold war, we had talked for hours on end, pausing only to buy bunches of tightly clustered and unbelievably sweet seedless grapes, and to observe the equally unbelievably fat ladies who lumbered around the beach and the shallow waters in scant black bikinis. I had never seen such rolls of flesh, let alone women confident enough to flaunt themselves naked on a public beach. I didn't really need my skills with the Russian language to ask for what we wanted – that was simply expressed as *chai* and more *chai* – but my vocabulary came in useful to decipher his bitter tirades about spoilt English girls expecting miracles from hard-working men just because they came sightseeing from the pampered West.

'How can you be starving on a train?' he'd grumble. 'In twenty-four hours your resistance is gone. You are a hamburger! You are easy food, too many clothes on your back. I know what hunger is,' he told me. 'Hunger is when you don't feel anything in your belly, not even pain any more. Hunger is when your legs and your eyes hurt.' He was a man of many words and much experience, and it seemed there was a part of his memory that, when tapped, had a lot to say, not because it was in any way dangerous, but just because what he remembered seemed to hurt and disturb him. I was the clock-key that set him chiming. I'd say, '*Chai*,' and he'd start up on an endless litany of hardship and shortage in his past. Then, after a few moments, he'd shake his head, as though suddenly remembering that he was a government official, and apologise gruffly, and then explain that the memory of Stalingrad always unsettled his brain. The mention of the siege itself was the trigger to start bartering. He knew his tea had to be paid for, because it wasn't part of the service as such, but he also knew that he wouldn't take a bribe, saying he hadn't survived so long only to go and do a stupid thing like that. At the end of each session he'd give me two glasses of tea, and not as a token of my thanks, but as a little something for his children, I'd give him whatever I could from our luggage, by which I mean whatever Joanna could bear to part with. In Leningrad, during the siege, the local people had boiled the leather from their shoes and belts to drink the broth and keep themselves alive. 'That was after the pets and the rats had been eaten, and all the rotten grain in the city.' I thought of those shoes and the rat queues and I felt tremendously guilty about the war. Guilty for not having known of the two million men who died as cannon fodder, for not having ever heard of the millions of civilians who died fighting back the Germans, starving themselves so that the Germans too would starve. What little I'd heard of the Russians before had put them in a menacing light. I'd thought they were people who threatened, not really people at all, especially not ones who had suffered. The word was that they were England's enemy. I had never even heard that they were our allies during the war, fighting not us but the Nazis just eighteen years before, and that every home had a shelf of photographs of smiling, buried faces. So when the old man scolded me, I could only agree. What he said was true: I was an ignorant, spoilt fool. But I still wanted tea. And although I would have gladly boiled down my shoes by the time we got to Warsaw, I was wearing sensible Clarks sandals with rubber soles, and not even penitents can eat rubber.

At Warsaw the train was due to stop for half an hour. I had a collection of foreign coins for my sisters, and by sifting through these I found enough Polish zlotys to run down the platform and purchase some food at a stall. Joanna was against even trying to do this, on the grounds that I might miss the train. She followed me down the platform on the inside corridor and then stood with a door held open, half hanging out, while I went for a sandwich. My little heap of coins wasn't enough for a sandwich, but the doughnuts were incredibly cheap and I bought three and then ran back aboard. In fact, the train left earlier than I'd been told, but it was all right, and better, because, after all, chocolate doughnuts are my favourite food. These were dark with thin white icing and raspberry jam inside, and they were incredibly fresh. If, like Fabrizio, Prince of Salina, I were to make up a general balance sheet of my whole life, 'trying to sort out of the immense ash-heap of liabilities the golden flecks of happy moments', it would definitely include the minute that it took me to eat my doughnut and a half as the train pulled out of the capital of ĆWZ Land.

All through Germany I made forays down the train, greeting those of my fellow passengers who showed any interest in me or spoke either Russian or English. The average greeting was, 'Hello, how are you?' followed up by, 'You are English, why do you speak Russian, do you have any bath plugs?' 'No.' 'Biro pens?' 'No.' 'That's a pity, nor do we.' Russian men can draw out their family photographs as quickly as the Sundance Kid could draw a gun. What did I think? It's hard to know what to say to a suddenly produced photograph, let alone think. 'They're beautiful,' became my stock reply. One man had the grace to laugh when I said this about his two lugubrious bespectacled children. 'I'm their father. I love them, and I don't think they're beautiful.' A lot of people had transistor radios, and most of them were tuned to a crackly jazz station. I think they were more status symbols than functional. A lot of the newly arrived Polish passengers in the second- and third-class wagons wanted to talk, but they weren't as keen as they were principled and wouldn't sink a lifelong policy of not understanding Russian, so we couldn't even get on photograph terms.

At Bromberg the shrivelled, scolding guard began to pack, as he'd be leaving the train at the German frontier. The thought of going home seemed to have cheered him up.

'I gave you a hard time,' he said, with what might have been a smile. 'You didn't give me a dollar, a sterling. It was nothing to you, for me, that is a lot.'

I explained that even in the West there was poverty, but found it hard to explain how poor people came to be travelling first class. For a moment he looked disappointed, almost ready to start again on his famine spiel.

'My mother has no man,' I said quickly, and then blushed for feeling that I had to excuse anything Joanna did or said.

'Out there,' he said, pointing down the corridor but

37

referring to Europe beyond the Wall, 'you are mean, mean in your hearts. We always have something,' he told me, thumping his frail chest. 'Even when we have nothing, we have something, something not even the Communist Party can take away. We are not mean.'

He paused, and continued ramming the socks and bras and my Black Watch tartan kilt into a very battered cloth bag. He pulled out the kilt and handed it back to me.

'I cheated you,' he admitted, 'but only because you are mean.' Then he handed me back a collection of rather grubby underclothes, saying, 'Your mother's things, take them back to her, your things you will manage without.'

He was brewing again in his samovar, and he served up two glasses of tea, embellished now with the real thing, slivers of lemon and a globule of black cherry jam. All through the journey, he had been wheedling for a Marks and Spencer cardigan. Marks and Spencer labels were as precious and desired as original Paris models. I had one in my suitcase, but I'd pretended otherwise until now. I think he knew that I had one, could sense, like a water-diviner in a desert, its valuable presence. I drank my tea and tried to give him back the kilt, but he refused, which was a shame because he might have liked it and I didn't. Then I went back to our blue-cushioned cabin and explained to Joanna that the ogre had relented and given me free *chai* and all her bras back. She hadn't been in on the bartering or the lecturing and so couldn't know what a triumph this was for East–West relations. I pulled out my suitcase and unpacked the hidden jumper. When I gave it to him, he didn't, I am glad to say, kiss me, but he kissed it and cuddled it like a small lost child in his arms. Then he remembered who he was, and handed it back to me solemnly. We argued as bitterly as we had done before until, relenting, he took the jumper and stuffed it in his bag.

The frontier guards were sour, grey-uniformed Germans. They burst into our cabin without knocking and immediately began shouting. Years of having her fingers stretched and rapped by the nuns at her German convent and a vivid memory of the London blitz welled up in Joanna, and she started to laugh. Gone were the days when one could be taken out on the platform and shot for this, although the Customs guard seemed sorry about such an unnecessary curbing of his powers. All he could do was stand and fix her with a glacial stare while his younger assistants waited uneasily behind him. Joanna was, by now, giggling uncontrollably as she finally exorcised the German influence on her education.

4

The moving metal and the mobile taps

Before I went to Russia, I dreamt of luxury; afterwards, I had memory to mix with my dreams. It is ironic that my first real taste of wealth came from a country usually associated with grim, unending queues and grey, cramped functionality. But so it was, and I returned to my dreary, colourless suburb of London filled not so much with a desire as with a need to be surrounded by fine silks and beautiful ceilings. It was, I suppose, the nearest I would get to an ambition, but never enough of one to strive for, since I believed that it would just happen, as stranger things have done, and fall like the gentle rain from heaven. (This was all in the days before Chernobyl, or acid rain, when one could rely on the weather, and since I lived in England I knew I could always rely on it to rain.)

I took no steps, therefore, towards obtaining my goal, but I read a lot of poetry and visited the palm house at Kew Gardens as often as I could. And when a perfect stranger called Don Jaime Terán stopped me on the corner of the notorious Abbeville Road and spoke to me in a language I didn't understand, but mentioned two words that needed no translation, I put up no resistance, and married him, in my sixteenth year, not so much for his offer of marriage itself as because of those two words, 'Italy' and 'Venezuela', and his invitation to go there with him.

Joanna had always spoken very ill of marriage, and advised us all against it. Her own mother had married just after the First World War and been separated from her husband shortly afterwards. Since her opinion of the institution was nothing short of vitriolic, and had been borne out by Joanna's own not infrequent experiments in the field, the incentive to go to Italy must have been very strong indeed to have overcome my early prejudices. Joanna's prejudices were also overcome, but not for the same reason. She simply believed in Jaime, as though he were in some way super-natural. Perhaps we both tended to feel that if one was going to marry a complete stranger, then he should at least be beautiful, and exceptional, and madly in love. I didn't, at the time I married him, know of his exceptional wealth, but even if I had, no fortune, or lack of it, could have outweighed the lure of his 'vamos a Italia'.

I never had the time with Jaime to tire of his ideas or demands, or even the chance to disagree with him. There was no bickering and no dissent, because he spoke only Spanish, and I, at first, spoke none, and later not enough to in any way hold my ground. Thus we began our marriage in a communion of silence, alleviated by our consultations with an atlas and the recitation of place names. The marriage itself was real enough, but it seemed like a mere piece of paper and my mother's much worn ring; it was our map-readings, ranging from Norway to Persia and across the Caribbean, that were invested with ritual solemnity. I was a poet who had never published so much as a haiku, but I was being offered perpetual motion, a life on a train. So I signed on the dotted line and packed my bags for the Continent, never to return.

That was not to be the last time that I left my native shores for good. In fact, in future years, I emigrated so often that even I no longer believed in my escapes. From what? From whom? It didn't matter, there was something about the state of mind, the readiness to abandon everything, the melo-drama of bidding these shores farewell. There is also something very attractive about a long farewell: the word itself implies so much more than simply goodbye. In Italian people say *ciao*, and they say *arrivederci*, but they never use the word *addio*, which would be the equivalent of farewell, or adieu. I asked why, and was told that *ciao* is for everyday, both a greeting and a goodbye, and *arrivederci* is for when someone goes away and one hopes to see them again, but when someone goes for so long that *arrivederci* cannot apply, one does not wish them *addio*. Why not? Ah, because in that case one would not send them to God, but to *va fan culo*. Rude, but appropriate.

When I left Charing Cross station, aged sixteen, set to conquer the world, Joanna wept and made me promise not to lose touch, and to write, to eat, to take care of my still precarious health. I didn't know, couldn't say, when I'd be back, if ever. My departure was shrouded in mystery and tears. I had enough books with me to last a long time. Jaime carried these, cursing at their weight and my vanity, since I was also taking with me a wardrobe of particularly heavy Edwardian gowns.

Two weeks later, we returned, a little chagrined, to Clapham. We had got as far as Paris, but had run out of money. Jaime, it seemed, was even more impractical than I. A month later we left again, this time with through tickets to Rome. This time Joanna didn't cry, fully expecting to see us home a few days later. We were gone for nearly two years, two years of drifting and hiding that were the reality of my so-called honeymoon.

I was a mere groupie in those days: an inept and often unwelcome addition to the group. My husband was a political exile who lived on the run (wanted by Interpol not for himself but for his two friends who travelled with us) and was pining for his ancestral sugar plantation in the Venezuelan Andes. He was an 'older man', charming, but deeply eccentric. Waving aside all the usual niceties of a relationship, he was content merely to marry me and then keep me with him, like a huge pot of syrup in his larder, stored up against any possible future disaster. He had a very sweet tooth. His best friend, also a charming man but afflicted by galloping neurasthenia at short notice and for long periods of time, loathed me. At the time, I was amazed and hurt that anyone could dislike me. With hindsight, I can see that there were a number of contributing factors, some of which only time could cure – namely, that I was very young and very silly and very ignorant. Now that I am no longer very young, and somewhat less ignorant, but still, alas, rather silly, the former exile and I are good friends. I can see, when he explains, how extraordinarily irritating, not to say alarming, it was for him to arrive at the Gare de Lyon after a morning spent strolling round Paris or visiting the Petit Palais, with his flayed nerves fractionally calmed and adjusted, to catch sight of me across the station concourse making my way to platform 12 and the Chiasso train.

He and his fellow exile were wanted for their involvement in the civil uprising in Venezuela of the sixties, an uprising that had almost amounted to a civil war. Now the two of them were in hiding, and he with the lacerated nerves was wanted for questioning, dead or alive. His companion was wanted dead. There are many ways of questioning political prisoners in South America, none of them pleasant. My husband's neurasthenic friend had already been on the receiving end of many such methods of questioning and had no desire to return for a final bout. Thus he made himself as inconspicuous as he could. His young friend, with a contract for his life hanging over him like a sinister halo at all times, had an extraordinary ability to pass through life in a way that was almost invisible. When people met him, under one of his many false names, as someone to drink or eat with, they could never describe what he looked like afterwards.

In deference to the danger of his two friends, my husband also assumed as much anonymity as a tall and naturally elegant man can. The idea was to glide through France and Italy as a nondescript group of travellers. In no way could my voluminous ankle-length yellow and black tartan travelling dress fit into this plan. I had read about the original garment in a Victorian novel and had instantly coveted such a robe. I had a replica made, enormous sleeves and all, and the rather astounding result was my favourite travelling attire. It needed no coat, and because it was pure wool it served for both summer and winter.

The Venezuelans begged me not to wear it. They hid it, they spilt things on it, they bribed me with any other clothes I might want. But I was headstrong in that matter alone. There was no constant point in my life, no rock past which I would not slip. I agreed to whatever plans emerged with craven servitude. I never argued, I never complained. I asked for nothing, and, partly because of my shyness, I contributed very little, either to them or to the world in general. I was a teenager quite incapable of going through the usual stages of social intercourse, marooned on an island of shyness, blushing not only when I had to speak to people, but also if I thought there was any possibility that someone might speak to me. My Venezuelan husband had seen me in the street, chosen me, followed me and then courted me with the tenacity of a limpet until I agreed to marry him. Had he not insisted as he did, I would still have been sitting shyly in London reading Victorian novels and dreaming of Byron. I had been traipsing around in Edwardian costumes since the age of twelve. The first came from a theatrical company's unwanted wardrobe. Later, designs were copied and made up from prints and magazines. Ashamed at my inability to argue or reason, ashamed of my ignorance, ashamed of my lack of social grace, it seemed that the only way of showing that I, too, had a mind and a will, and that although my passport already said 'poet' for my profession and raised many a laugh, one day I would indeed become one. One day I would be known as something other than a potential misalliance. So I was headstrong over my clothes, and I championed my yellow tartan travelling gown as though my life depended on my wearing it, blind to the fact that two people's lives really might depend on my not wearing it.

When, finally, after those two years, Jaime was pardoned for his part in the guerrilla war, he took me back to the semi-feudal land of his birth, to Venezuela. His estate spanned miles of hills and valleys, and it was hard to reach and virtually impossible to leave.

During the seven years that I spent in Venezuela, the nearest I came to a train was describing one to the peasant workers on the Hacienda Santa Rita where I lived. Venezuela had oil and an iron ore mountain, and it had precious stones embedded in its rocks, and luscious plants surging out of its lands. It had the Angel Falls, the biggest waterfall in the world, discovered by a crashed American pilot, Jimmy Angel, in the fifties, and it had roads, many of them built by the former dictator, Pérez Jiménez, that equalled any North American highway in their complexity and girth. Venezuela was the birthplace of Simón Bolívar the liberator both of Venezuela itself and then of most of Latin America. Venezuela had all this, and more, but it had no railways.

My cousin by marriage, Luís Daniel Terán, was an engineer who worked for a while reconstructing the country's one token line that ran from Barquisimeto and then quickly petered out into nowhere, the tracks stopping where the initial enthusiasm flagged so many years before. Luís Daniel told me that when the rare trains did run on this distant line, people still threw sticks and stones at them, or jumped in front, rather as they did on that first run from Stockton to Darlington in 1815.

However, on the Hacienda Santa Rita, anything further away than Timotes in the uplands, and Trujillo in the other direction, was regarded as a kind of mass fantasy, and thus, really, disregarded. For the people of the Cañada de Mendoza where I lived, anyone who came from farther away than Mendoza Fría up the road, or Carmania on the far frontier of the Terán plantation, was a foreigner, and foreigners were vastly less interesting than Mendoceros, as they called themselves. Their interest in each other's lives was so intense that a whole network of gossip and information passed across the hills and valleys of the hacienda almost telepathically. No one could pee behind a tree without the whole estate knowing exactly which tree it was and what shade of yellow the urine had been. There was a herbalist in Carmania who diagnosed anything and everything from urine samples, and this made the hacienda's collective waterworks a topic of much discussion.

Although my movements on the estate were closely monitored, and every word I spoke was somehow relayed to all and sundry, however privately I had thought them spoken, as an outsider I merited very little direct interest in my first year there. I was not only an outsider, but a *misiua*. *misius* were Europeans, but they could just as easily have been Martians, since there was no knowledge of what or where Europe, or, come to that, any of the rest of Venezuela or the world, actually lay. Word travelled back to the hacienda from Valera, the nearest town and the place where the workers sometimes went to market, that this was what I was. In the thirties, one Mr Lee, a Chinese man from Trinidad (which was English, and England was in Europe, which made Mr Lee and me virtually cousins), had settled, no one could remember why, in Valera. A lot of people kept canaries locally and bred them for the sweetness of their song. This infamous *misiu* had also bred canaries, bringing with him strains of the bird that were vastly superior to any of the local inbred varieties, and had refused to let his neighbours' songbirds mate with his. Mr Lee had been mean. Thus all *misius* were potentially mean. During all the years that I lived there, I was never quite forgiven for the canaries.

There was also a Russian lady, known as La Rusa, who ran a brothel on the outskirts of the town. It was rumoured that La Rusa actually came from Maracaibo and assumed her accent to add mystique to her establishment, but nobody knew this for sure, and the workers never travelled as far as these outskirts of the town, and if they had, they wouldn't have had the money to visit the brothel, so it was all irrelevant really to the geography of Europe versus Santa Rita.

When, after two years, I gave birth to *la niña Iseult*, literally 'the child Iseult', the foreman of the estate sent his daughter, Coromoto, ostensibly to help. Coromoto's help, however, consisted largely of sifting through the contents of my four painted trunks and asking questions about everything in them. It was she who first learnt that Don Jaime, my husband, and I had travelled to Santa Rita on a ship. She had never seen or heard of an ocean, and the notion of a ship was quite fascinating to her. It took a great deal of ingenuity to explain the concept of an ocean's vastness, and all we could come up with was a great patchwork river. I don't think Coromoto ever really believed in the ship as a means of travel or as anything other than a figment of my imagination. But she grew to like my descriptions of things, and gradually I told her of other curiosities like televisions and telephones and trains. It was the train that most caught her fancy. And it was the story of the train that she took home with her one

Sunday, back to the long wattle and daub hut where her parents and brother lived.

When she returned after her afternoon off, she did so accompanied by a delegation of small children who all wanted to hear about this train. So I described it again, its size and speed and how it ran on iron tracks and had running water inside it. None of the workers had piped water in their houses. At best, they had cut bamboo channels to bring water from springs in the hills down to a barrel in their cluttered yards; at worst, they gathered water from, and bathed in, one of the many streams that flowed through the hacienda. Over the years, the children leaked their stories to their elders, and occasionally one of the workers, and even the foreman himself, came into the Casa Grande to be told of the moving metal and the mobile taps.

Meanwhile, the country's commerce continued to be transported exclusively by road, and juggernauts careered and crashed all over the Andes as they did elsewhere in Venezuela. Along the edge of every road, small wooden crosses marked the spot were somebody had died. On one particular stretch, known as *las curvas de San Pablo*, on the road, ironically, to Barquisimeto (where the token railway track was installed), the crosses were so frequent that in many places they made a low fence.

I've often thought that if I had sixpence for every time someone has said to me, 'What a lovely sun-tan you've got, where did you get it?' I'd be a rich lady. When I returned from Venezuela, a new catch-phrase occurred. This time it was, 'Seven years in South America, how wonderful!' followed inevitably by streams of praise for Machu Picchu, or Buenos Aires, or Rio de Janeiro, or anywhere else, but never anywhere I'd actually been to. The assumption was always that my seven years had been spent travelling around the continent, rather than travelling around the parameters of a sugar plantation. When I explained that I had been farming, the assumption still remained: surely, in my holidays, I had been to see this and that, at least? I would try, in vain, to explain that there were no holidays on a semi-feudal sub-tropical sugar estate. Elsewhere, crops are harvested and rotated and allowed to grow in natural cycles. But sugar is planted on a two-weekly rota, and then, a year later, cut field by field on a two-weekly rota. The sugar factory, or *trapiche*, took two weeks to process all the cane and turn it into packed and graded muscovado sugar. Travel was from the Casa Grande to the sugar mill, or, more pleasurably, across the hills of the hacienda.

Sometimes I would manage to delegate the running of the estate, and the workers, and the house, and the care of Iseult, and the sheep, cows, hens, pigs etc., for a couple of days. It was six hundred kilometres to Caracas, and our lorry-loads of avocado pears had to go there to be sold. So between April and August, when the avocado harvest began and then continued, staggered by variety, to last as long as possible to meet the constant demand, I'd go with one of the lorry-drivers to the capital, and that, in itself, seemed like an achievement in tactical strategy. The avocados discoloured, once picked, in the sun, so the journeys had to be made overnight. This allowed at least a day in the city, while the driver slept. Sometimes I'd manage to squeeze in an extra twenty-four hours there, but the chaos on my return would rarely be worth the extra night of razzle on the town.

When I finally left Venezuela, leaving behind me a marriage that I could no longer live with and a great deal of regret, I also took the notion of a train as being somehow symbolic of all that is wonderful and amusingly unreal. After seven years of watching sugar-cane grow through its cycles and tending avocado pears from one rainy season to the next, and then nursing them through the intermittent droughts, I felt a great urge to see things differently, but most of all to see different things.

Thus it was as a repressed member of the fun squad that I arrived in Paris and unleashed myself on the boulevards, determined to be as irresponsible as I could. I wanted something really exciting to happen to me. I wasn't sure what, but I wanted to be wild. After two weeks of flattering and unflattering attentions to myself and my daughter, a would-be film director with a strange stare followed me down the rue de Vaugirard and tried to strangle me in the corridor of my hotel. I fainted, and he left. Then I came round, and I left, at midnight, for Berlin with Iseult, and our two suitcases, and the bag of money that was all I had brought out of the rich till of the hacienda. For the next five months I zigzagged from Paris to London and Berlin, where I'd met a handsome, winsome architect who sweetened my existence a great deal more than the hundreds of tons of sugar I had made in the Andes. I avoided Andean justice and strangely staring stranglers as best I could, and I made a note of all the South American places that people spoke of with such awe, determined to return there expressly so that I too might see the glorious sights.

5

From England to the Amazon and Patagonia and back again

I had planned an incredibly complicated route, consisting of twenty-two flights and a number of rail-journeys and links. As it emerged, during the course of my trip, the travel arrangements were about the only things I had planned, and I travelled from one country to another with a mixture of blissful and calamitous ignorance. The climax of my journey was to be two weeks going from Buenos Aires deep into Patagonia by train and then back to a place called Jujuy. From the age of four, when I first read of the extinct Patagons, and then, much later, reading W. H. Hudson, it had been my ambition to visit Patagonia. Second to that, I wanted to go to the Andes. At school, when the time came to think of a career, I had borne these Latin American longings clearly in mind, and chose to study archaeology so that one day, some day, I could find an excuse for going to those two places. I didn't believe, in my youth, that a writer could live by the pen, and so I lined up this alternative career to finance the other.

It was 1978 and I was twenty-five. I began my journey in what was once Dutch Guiana, next door to British Guiana, my vicarious homeland. Surinam was hot, and the language incomprehensible. I stayed at the Hotel Krasnapolsky, an amazing wooden palace where I made friends with a brilliant blue-eyed businessman who spoke fifteen languages and loved poetry and pretty girls. My next stop was Cayenne, in French Guiana. This, too, was hot, and the language, French Creole, was also incomprehensible. I struggled by with a very limited vocabulary of essential sentences like, 'Another gin and tonic please,' and, 'When is the next plane to Belém?' It seemed that there was no end to the number of gin and tonics

I might consume, but the next plane to Belém was not until Wednesday. I lost count of my drinking tally some time on Monday, and I staggered on to a small jungle hopper on Wednesday morning feeling that as well as all the heavy farming, my spell in the Venezuelan Andes had taught me to drink most of the world under the table. It was a small achievement but one that I felt proud of, after years of apprenticeship and being sick.

The plane circled over the notorious but deserted Devil's Island on its way to the Amazon, and then landed in a heat haze at Belém. A military staff car drove up to the steps of the plane, and the officer and two armed guards in it waited until I touched the tarmac, whereupon I was escorted into their car and driven out of the city. All the officer had said to me was, in Portuguese, 'This is no place for you.'

I mumbled something about being in transit to São Paulo, but by then the officer was staring out of the car window into the middle distance, taking less notice of me than he did of a small midge hovering frantically over his side window. I was taken to a four-star hotel on the outskirts of the jungle capital of Belém. Nothing more was said in the car, but as I was escorted through the luxurious hotel lobby, the single word 'passport' was snapped in my direction.

I was brought up to believe that one didn't argue when this could be avoided by the gentle exercise of good manners. I made my way as elegantly as I could through the palms and the Louis Quinze furniture of the lobby, frogmarched between the two green-eyed gorillas who formed my guard. As we neared the lift, I recalled long nights in the Quartier Latin in Paris listening to the exiles and the escapees and the refugees discussing the pros and cons and strengths of the various police forces across the continent of South and Central America. Brazil was always at the bottom of the league. There were never many Brazilians there, presumably because not many survived their stays in native jails to tell the tale. But enough horror stories remained to make me hand over my passport with the most gracious obsequiousness. I have always had a very childish voice, which, at the best of times, scarcely rises above a whisper. There, it was little more than a squeak. I touched a potted orchid as I passed into the lift, telling myself I might never have another chance to enjoy the feel of petals on my fingers, and ventured a high-pitched, appreciative, 'Que beleza!'

The officer in charge gave me an unequivocal look. The plant, apparently, was not a *beleza*. I was ready to sign an affidavit to this effect as we hummed up in the lift to the eleventh floor. By the time we entered a large, lavishly furnished double room I had to pinch my arm to stop myself saying what an ugly, repulsive orchid it had been. I had decided to say nothing, remembering that Jaime, who had spent two years as a political prisoner in Venezuela and four months in an interrogation camp, maintained that the best policy was to say nothing at first, and then to talk helpful drivel and hope for a change of government. There was no question of my being raped: I had such a craven fear of being tortured that I would have given myself to the officer, the guards and the orchid.

We stood by the picture window for about five minutes, staring down at the flowering palm trees and the hibiscus bushes in the garden. Not a word was spoken. I concentrated so hard on the hibiscus petals that black dots formed in front of my eyes. Then my chief captor turned on his heel, clicked his boots together and bowed slightly.

'This is for your own good,' he told me, again in Portuguese. With shades of the Inquisition in my mind, I didn't find his words in the least bit reassuring. He left, and I found myself alone in a large room with a television and a fridge full of miniature bottles of wines and spirits. On further investigation I discovered a tray of frozen chocolate bars, several packets of salted cashew nuts, and a telephone. When I tried my door, it was unlocked, but one of the guards, still armed with a machine gun, stood outside it. He waved me back in. I telephoned reception, and a charming young girl offered me a room-service lunch. I asked for an outside line, and was told that I could have anything I wanted in my room, but no other contact. For the next two days nothing changed except the guard outside my door. I didn't know what to do, so I did nothing. The television provided an almost non-stop barrage of local soap operas, long shrill affairs about slaves and cowboys and *meninas* in corsets having hysterics on Louis Quinze sofas in the Amazon basin a hundred years ago. It calmed my nerves to watch their televised carousel of emotions, and I was surprisingly comfortable there. The food was exquisite, and I ordered about nine meals a day just to fill in my time.

After two days that seemed infinitely longer, my kidnapper returned and escorted me back to the airport. He gave me my passport, and smiled, and helped me on to a plane to São Paulo. I was so relieved to be leaving with my face unscarred that I didn't even ask what it had been about. I half feared he had forgotten, and might suddenly remember. So I sat on my window seat of the plane watching the antics of another small midge, and thinking, 'What, still alive at twenty-two?' I was actually a little older, but ladies are allowed to fictionalise their age, and were they not, no one could stop them.

At São Paulo, I was almost the last person to disembark, and I did so reluctantly, with my knees knocking against my typewriter case. I'd been given all my luggage back at the airport. I crossed the tarmac, sweating from stomach cramps, and fighting with a nervous diarrhoea. No one was waiting for me there, and none of the many guards showed the least interest in me, except, now and then, to whistle at my legs. I eyed their machine guns cautiously and then spent as long as I dared washing my hands and combing my hair in the Ladies. When the fifty-minute wait was finally through, the plane to Rio was delayed for ten hours and I had no alternative but to wait in the transit lounge and muse on life and love and the ephemeral beauty of the orchid. I wondered what Byron would have said, had he come to Brazil. Though, of course, he would have had to come at the time of the slaves and the cowboys and the corseted hysteria. 'Let there be light!' says God, and there was light! 'Let there be blood!' says man, and there's a sea.

At some point during this wait I drank a glass of warm milk and took my cardigan off, and although neither of these occasions may seem worth mentioning, the latter was the cause of my making two new friends on the flight. It was going to be hot in Rio, and I had brought a plastic bag with me to put a cardigan or jumper in and take out again at will as the weather changed on my hop-scotch flights. As I queued up, rigid with paranoia after my recent sojourn at the four-star hotel, waiting to board the plane, two Englishmen leapt out of the queue and embraced me. They explained that they had just spent four months in the interior, and the sight of my John Lewis bag had stirred them into a mood of nostalgia blended with hilarity. They insisted that we sit together and swap stories of Oxford Street and Piccadilly Circus, interspersed with appreciative sighs, and scrambled eggs and coffee, and interjections like 'Marks and Spencer', and 'Boots', and 'Aquascutum', and 'Charing Cross'. Each of these pronouncements would be met by profound nods from the others as we wallowed in our nostalgia. I didn't dare admit that I had only been travelling a week and really didn't feel any deprivation comparable to theirs of such places as Boots and Woolworth's; they seemed drunk on their memories of shops they hadn't seen for a long time and maybe hadn't thought to see again.

By Rio, we had become such fast friends that the two invited me to postpone my ongoing flight from Rio to Buenos Aires and stay with them for a few days. When I refused, they offered to pay for my every expense, but I still refused, deterred not so much by lack of funds as by the memory of my two days under guard outside Belém and a strong inclination to get out of Brazil as fast as possible, before the immaculate captain changed his mind and sent for me again. As we neared our destination, my companions became more and more insistent on my staying, unravelling a tale of future revelry in the city if only I would consent. The scrambled eggs had long been cleared away, and in their place were a startling number of miniature bottles of Scotch and gin. I was half tempted to hit Rio in the manner which they described. They both knew it well, and promised huge meals and dancing. As we landed, they tried one last onslaught on my stubborn refusals, but I was adamant, and we disembarked and went our different ways, they with Rio tumbling at their feet, and I with my green and white polythene bag.

While fighting my many court cases in England on the one hand, and sifting my way through the soup of Berlin nightlife and readjusting from being a farmer in the outback to being an unoccupied single person with a suitcaseful of manuscripts on the other, I had become engaged to an Argentinian geologist called Hans who, although he lived in South America, didn't live in the Argentine but had decided to travel down to show me his native land. We had arranged, weeks before, that he would meet me at my next stop, Ezeiza airport in Buenos Aires, whence we would travel down the tail of the Andes through Patagonia to the land of W. H. Hudson, and on past there into a wilderness of colour and stone.

I hadn't seen him for some months, so it was with great excitement that I stumbled down the steps of the plane to greet him. Then, it seemed, all the canaries of Buenos Aires were loaned, and sang the sweetest cross-bred songs they'd ever sung.

The Patagonian Express left for Zapala a week later. Hans and I took a hamper of cold steaks and grapes, several bottles of wine, a bottle of brandy and a chess set to occupy our time. It was to be a journey of five days on the train, extended by ten days of stopping over into a fortnight. Our first stop was Zapala, also known as the 'Windy City' (Ciudad del Viento). Hans had a map of Patagonia that faded down into the South Arctic sea below Tierra del Fuego. There was also a pair of tiny dots marking a group of islands called Las Malvinas. I had already wrecked a dinner party by never having heard of them (this, remember, was well before the war) and then, on having a map produced over the steaks and broccoli, by saying, 'Oh, you mean the Falklands!' Some of the guests were so offended that they got up and left. So much for ignorance. But the map had many other names – Rosario, Córdoba, Avellaneda, Tandil and Bahía Blanca, San Carlos de Bariloche and, further south, Comodoro Rivadavia,

Neuquén and on and on to the Tierra del Fuego, the wild and desolate kingdom of the ancient Patagons.

As we rattled out of the station we drank brandy and played chess. I play this game with an impulsive, throw-away manner which occasionally wins me a match against far more skilful opponents, so disturbed by my recklessness that they imagine there must be a plan that they cannot fathom behind my moves. As the railway tracks cut through vineyards on either side, a man with a face so red it looked scalded moved from the otherwise empty seats across the gangway from us and sat down beside Hans and directly opposite me. I moved my bishop into a perilous position on the board.

'That's what I do,' the man announced in Spanish.

I had never come across anyone who played chess as consistently and as badly as I do, and so I registered some surprise.

'Yes, I'm a farmer,' he said. 'Grapes. All grapes.'

Hans had little desire to discuss grapes, and so he moved his queen, threatening both to take my bishop and to mate my king with his next turn.

'I used to be a farmer,' I told the intruder, while studying the maze of burst capillaries in his cheeks.

'Grapes?' he asked hopefully.

'Sugar.'

'Grapes are the thing,' he assured me.

I moved my bishop to a similarly endangered position. Hans shifted a knight to threaten it, but the red-faced farmer shook his head sadly and moved the piece elsewhere on the board.

'Grapes are the thing,' he repeated.

Hans, with gritted teeth and whitened knuckles, moved his knight back, not seeming to realise that in married life, 'three is company and two is none.'

'Sugar is a noble crop,' I argued. This was what people always said of sugar on the hacienda in Venezuela. After some years of trial and error there, I decided that it really was a noble crop because one could plant it upside down, forget about it for a year, starve it and trample it, and it would still flourish like a perennial weed.

'Ah,' he sighed wisely. 'But grapes are grapes.'

I moved a pawn to release my imprisoned rook. For the first time, Hans and the farmer seemed to agree. It was a bad move, one that proved to be the first link in a chain of slaughter.

The wooden pieces went back into their travelling case. Hundreds more vineyards whizzed past the windows. Hans slept fitfully while the grape-man tried to persuade me, as one farmer to another, that the only plant worth putting in the soil is a vine. It became more of a crusade than a conversation: the heathen cane of the hacienda must go, and the lands be rebaptised with the vine. Every time I got a chance to fit a word or two into his dissertation, I mentioned that I no longer owned any land and therefore had no say in its produce.

'No, you have influence, you must have influence, you are a woman. Vines are like women. See how they cling and climb, gnarled old women, young fresh virgins – all knotted together, and bearing juicy fruits.' There was a long pause as he regained his composure, wiping the sweat from his crimson brow. 'Cut them back, prune the shoots, back to the bare bones, like women!'

Hans was, by now, fast asleep, probably, I began to feel, the most sensible course. The farmer's passions were roused to such a degree that I feared for my own extremities. He paused again and brooded. The train slowed and grunted into a station.

'San Rosario,' he said, and stood up. He had a tartan suitcase with a label from Harrods. (I had noticed that there was a branch in Buenos Aires.) He banged this several times with the flat of his massive raw hand. 'Grapes,' he said again, as though I might have missed the gist of his previous forty-minute monologue. 'Remember that!' And he banged his suitcase lovingly, as if it were full of them, and left the train.

I moved across to look on to the platform. A number of equally apoplectic men were getting off and a number of new passengers were getting on. At each stop, the intake of people fell into a recognisable pattern. There would be farmers going to or coming from market, a few besuited civil servants, a priest or a nun, a handful of crop-headed conscripts and one or two unidentifiable travellers of both sexes.

The train moved on, and on. Night came, but the landscape remained unchanged. We ate cold steak sandwiches. Looking around the compartment, I noticed that everyone was eating cold steak sandwiches. Hans told me that in the Argentine everyone ate steak and meat in vast quantities, since that was what there was most of – beef and more beef. It was the poor man's crust. Bread was a luxury, meat was everywhere.

Argentina is so unlike Venezuela that it is hard to conceive of the two countries having anything in common, either socially, historically or geographically. It seems very European. Over half of the population are Italian by origin, but the atmosphere is redolent far more of the north than the south of Italy. There is something slightly Germanic about Buenos Aires itself, at its centre a hotbed of organisation and cleanliness. Venezuelans often dislike and despise Argentinians, and the feeling, I think, is mutual. The soft, slurring whispers of Argentinian Spanish are seen, further north, as an affectation, while the meticulous order and punctuality of the south is regarded with derision by the wild and chaotic tropical zones. Everything was different and novel to me, seen in the context of being a part of South America, a large chunk of Latin life. I sat in my seat, a cultural chameleon. Not Venezuelan and not Argentinian, and not needing to pass judgement or take sides with either one or the other. I was *ni chicha ni limonada*, as they used to say in the Andes (*chicha* being the fermented maize drink of the Indians, and lemonade the soft drink of the Spaniards).

The train turned tail, from north to south, and began its slow trail through the wheat and cattle of the Pampas, now in its antipodean winter. We slept our first night of the journey under a tartan travel rug, which also bore a label from the indigenous Harrods. Although it was a little chilly, I felt that we would have been warm enough with extra jumpers, but Hans knew better. He had been down this line before. On the second day the train moved into a red plain.

At first this seemed merely picturesque. Then, as we cut through the dust, a red film began to gather around the insides of the windows. Within half an hour, this had formed a layer covering the entire carriage. Gradually handkerchiefs and scarves were taken out all along the compartment, and people tied them over their noses and mouths like bandits getting ready for a raid. I had a fantasy that there was some fault in the windowpanes of our bit of the train, and I moved along to another section to see if there was any way of escaping the dust. The train was full of bandits and highwaymen, so I returned to my seat, and Hans and I huddled under the travelling rug, choking and gasping, for the next three hours, while a red landscape rushed by unseen.

We had decided to break the journey at San Carlos de Bariloche, a quaint summer ski resort that had long hosted the well-heeled skiers of the world. The main street was a Nordic huddle of Viennese tea rooms, German beer gardens, Scandinavian craft shops and Prussian delicatessens. There was a truly Swiss cleanliness about the place, and an air of Alpine jollity, and not so much as a trace or a wishbone of the Indians who once lived there but had been systematically wiped out to make way for the Argentinians.

The Argentine is almost totally European, except for the soil that covers the reluctant remains of the Indians who were ground into it to make way for the nineteenth-century prosperity, the beef and the wheat and the railway. There are Welsh villages and Gaelic villages as well as Swiss and Austrian villages, all havens for Europe's persecuted or poor minorities, but there are no Indian villages. Argentinians eat home-made Italian *gnocchi*, traditionally on Sundays, and they are proud of their racial tolerance – you will find no colour prejudice in Bariloche; in fact, you will find no coloured people there at all, not even the ones who belong there. Generations after the genocide, the *après-ski* sip purple hot chocolate and munch Sacher torte while discussing the inexhaustible wonders of the Pista Tronador, a volcanic crater filled with a minimum of thirty metres of snow where the most avid skiers can always find a dream slope for the perfect descent.

I felt almost offended by Bariloche. In Venezuela I had
seen the Colonia Tovar, a settlement of Black Forest peasants
whom the Wesler bank had enticed out there when they
bought Venezuela from the King of Spain and then abandoned
when they gave the country up as bad business. There,
incredibly inbred German peasants grew strawberries and
hops, and lived in grey stone streets, and served in grey stone
shops. But there, people went to gawp and wonder before
returning to their own, traditional, native life. Here, a steady
stamping had accompanied the folk dances and no other life
had been allowed. No wonder so many Nazis fled to the
Argentine after their Final Solution failed; here was a land
where an earlier one had worked. Notwithstanding, I was
lured by the splendour of the slopes, the darkness of the hot
chocolate and the gorgeousness of the cakes. At least these
Barilochans (with the exception of a few ex-Nazis who had
mixed and mingled out of view) were not the ones who had
committed the atrocities; it was also a long way from the left-
wing 'disappeared' of the big cities. It was a pretty town in a
pretty place, and all around it an almost supernatural
stillness beckoned one out into the wilderness of hills and
lakes that stretched away into the Patagonian desert.

Perhaps, had I been less of a wimp, I would have gone to
San Carlos de Bariloche to ski, like everyone else, but having a
pathological fear of breaking both or either of my lovely legs
I have never done more than climb, be carried, ferried, or
lifted to the top of any (in fact many) given slopes and then
refused to go down in the conventional way. Not even my
admiration for Sir Arthur Conan Doyle, who originally
popularised skiing as a sport, can induce me to risk my
shapely limbs. Shame and stubbornness never allow admission
of this craven fear until such time as it has become apparent,
in situ. And yet, on each new occasion, I believe that I shall
transform, miraculously, from quadriplegic to athlete at the
top of the piste.

With the usual mish-mash of bravado and deceit, I had not
actually told Hans that I wouldn't ski. When the day came, I
had confessed, but not dwelt on, the fact that I couldn't,
without admitting to being a jibbering idiot. Thus, while he

skied, I brooded, hundreds of metres up in the air. They were the best peaks I had ever wept on, and the snow was the softest and driest I had ever known.

After about three days of abortive fun of this sort, Hans capitulated, rather than continue to witness his idol blubbering. We went for a drive, and a long, long walk, and spent a day and night on the shores of a lake called Nahel Huapí.

Nahel Huapí was an ancient sacred place, a centre of myths and stillness. The lake itself was surrounded by boulders: huge, hump-backed stones in every imaginable hue of green, grey and purple. The dull sheen of their colours was like dusty jewels, hundreds and thousands of pink and purple gems, and the beach was laden with tons of opaque emeralds and amethysts and slate-grey, pigeon-necked, iridescent rocks rounded by a multi-million-year-old volcano, and left to guard the whispering lapping shores of the lake.

Further south, the landscape became bleaker, and the dry grass shorter, and the wind kept the low trees stunted, and an almost magical stillness seemed to rise up from the earth like mist. The keening of circling birds, the rustle of insects, the coloured drifting clouds, the many grey skies, sudden rainbows, staggering views, were all as nothing to Nahel Huapí. Or, rather, Nahel Huapí seemed to hold the secrets of all Patagonia. They were secrets whispered by the wild grasses to the pastel rocks, and held by the rocks for hundreds of millions of years, and held by them still, as silent as the lost tribes and the scattered swamp flowers.

6

From flirting and the Fens
to Italy

All men are intrinsical rascals and I am only sorry that, not being a
dog, I can't bite them.

All through my childhood, my father had been constantly
engaged to be married. Despite his frequent marriages, he
always seemed to be concurrently engaged to any number of
fiancées. In anyone less generous with himself (and by this, I
don't just mean from the waist down) it would have seemed
unbecoming. For Jan, it just seemed inevitable. He was
pursued, and succumbed, as he often told me, to few
temptations, considering how many he was presented with.
My potential stepmothers ranged from Australian diamond
heiresses to Italian countesses, English professors, Caribbean
dancers, African militants, a Canadian sculptress, an
American ambassador's wife, an anthropologist. There was
no end to them.

During my sojourn in Germany and my travels around
South America, I seemed to be emulating my dizzy papa. For,
while being still married in Venezuela, engaged to the
Argentinian and lingeringly involved in Berlin, I became
linked to London through the person of the Scottish poet
George MacBeth. We met at a literary salon in Cadogan
Square, and within a few months he had adopted my mother
(who, at the time, was flirting with death by means of a
bizarre blood disease), my six-year-old daughter and myself.

Our early romance took place between the corridors of St
Thomas's Hospital and the tea room of the Ritz. He fell in
love with me (and my to him heady, to me tedious, past),
while I fell in love with his brilliance and his total concern for

62

my triangular family. After years of talking sheep and avocados, legend and rot-gut rum, I had found someone who could not only talk about poetry, but write and read it like no other. I often felt that George would have liked to have been a pirate for the romance and the daring of the act. I think he thought I was, or had been, one. He made what had seemed to me meaningless years of violence, snakes and drudgery appear glamorous. He encouraged me to turn my short stories into novels, and I encouraged him to buy big houses.

For four years the Monopoly board was swept clear of other pieces while we renamed the streets with the convoluted names of semi-derelict mansions.

By a process of osmosis our work began to resemble each other's. Travelling became mostly a shuttling to and from poetry readings in England and America and occasionally abroad. We moved to Norfolk, made a Victorian maze in the garden, immersed ourselves in Victoriana, turning our literary profits into *objets d'art* and junk. Our public life was snowballing towards great things, and then, in 1984, what had initially brought us together dragged us apart. Joanna got cancer and, after a gruelling summer, went back to St Thomas's Hospital and died.

The parameters of my world caved in, and I sank, at first imperceptibly, into the mud. The year after my mother died, George and I had a son, Alexander, whose traumatic birth drained away whatever strength I had retained from losing Joanna. Within weeks of his birth, we bought a crumbling half-Tudor half-Victorian castle in the Norfolk Fens, and our passion for pretty ruins consumed us.

The manic energy I have always had, which, combined with skills acquired through years of close observation on the hacienda, had allowed me to restore our previous noble piles single-handed, now turned inwards. I no longer had the will to plaster, paint, patch and decorate twenty rooms, re-lay floors, install stoves, transform gardens and build walls. Instead, I felt the grey mould of the Fens settle on my mind. While interviewers flocked to tell me what a wonderful life I had, and how happy I must be, I hid my grief and became very British. I kept my upper lip stiff for two years and then bolted.

I have often gone back to the castle in Norfolk, stayed in and even lived there, and am very close to George, but our marriage ended, really, the day I set off for Italy and broke the spell.

Through all the funnelled madness of my depression I was obsessed by the idea of Italy. For almost two years I had looked out across the bleak flatlands of the Fens, watching the bare treeless expanses of clay mud peppered only by scattered bungalows and the distant glint of the sugar factory chimney. It seemed ironic that I, who had once been called the Queen of the Andes, with my endless miles of sugar-cane and the tallest chimney in the state, should have come to fester in the long shadow of a steel sugar-beet plant. The sporadic pounding of the pumping station that kept the outlying land from flood seemed to urge me to flee across the Alps to the Apennines.

I yo-yoed on the train from nearby Magdalen Road to another world in London, developing the family schizo-phrenia as I went. There was Downham Market, Littleport, Ely, and Cambridge, Audley End and London. Cambridge was where my parents fell in love; it was there that they both expiated their own breakdowns in a clinic that must have looked out over the bleak dark nothingness that is all that the Fens can mirror to a sick mind.

I kept myself alive by lunches, the famous free lunches that are supposed not to exist. Three times a week I lunched with three different friends; all close enough not to slip into the glitz of my new public image, but none of them close enough to see that under my placid smile I was getting ready to become a raving loony.

The trains from Liverpool Street run at two-hourly intervals towards King's Lynn. I used to metamorphose on those trains. By Audley End I would have calmed my manic spirits and the effect of the gin and tonics had begun to wear off. At Cambridge I would remind myself of the heritage and at Ely of my lot. I never had the heart to say, dear George, I am rotting away. It seemed so ungrateful, and, somehow, so ungracious. In fact, it was far more ungracious to wait until I found myself on the brink of suicide and then run away. At the time, my horror of disturbing the peace outweighed my judgement. I was, however, acutely aware of the irony of my situation. There I would be, in my castle in the Norfolk Fens, sipping tea or sherry in the reconstructed pre-Raphaelite interior, talking to interviewers from magazines and newspapers of varying quality about my so-called romantic lifestyle and being told what a wonderful, 'almost fairytale' life I had led. Wasn't I lucky! When would I write that thrilling autobiography?

I was only thirty. I wasn't prepared to have my life over, finished, reviewed as from a premature old age. When I looked out across the gardens, the herbaceous borders that I had planted stared back at me. They would take four years to mature. It was too long to wait, not least because they would mature just as well without me. Behind the crenellations I was growing out of touch with the world. When I looked through the thick windows across the dank black mud of the Fens, I just kept thinking I didn't want to be there. At the end of our woods, the church of Wiggenhall St Mary the Virgin stood proud with its squat tower and grotesque gargoyles defying the wind. Inside, it had the finest pew ends in Britain, saints and martyrs carved out of oak. Also inside was the alabaster tomb of the last of the Capravilles, the early Tudor owners of the house and manor. Under their prostrate figures was a line of tiny swaddled children, all their dead heirs, whom the bitter Fens had killed. Outside the church lay the graveyard with the tombs of all the many men and women and their children who had struggled under the battlements before me. Local children amused themselves by pulling off the alabaster hand of Sir Thomas de Capraville and waving it around the massive church interior. Shyer children merely scratched their initials on such worthy subjects as Saints Ann and Beatrice. Outside, the graveyard lay besieged by the wind which shared out the crop of crisp packets and chocolate wrappers, one day to this grave, and one day to that.

Meanwhile, back at St Mary's Hall, Batwoman was growing restless and the colony of bats inside the bathroom window-frame was driving her mad. Only the regular trips to London could lull her rising hysteria. Only that regular shunting of the Intercity 125 practising its steps as for a dance along the truncated platform of Magdalen Road could bring back any sense of reality to her slowly mouldering life. Magdalen Road is one of those stations closed by Beeching (who has a lot to answer for) in the sixties. What distinguishes it, politically, from so many other such stations, is that it was reopened by an act of Parliament in the seventies. Its platform is exactly two carriages long, and precision-halting is essential for all drivers there. If the guard's van is needed, then the whole train has to shunt along in order to pack in whatever isolated article is standing by. There is no ticket office, and the station is permanently unmanned. To descend there was always an act of faith. There were no taxis and no telephones and the village of Wiggenhall St Mary Magdalen (there are many Wiggenhalls in Norfolk) was a long hike down a winding blustery lane which seemed to lead nowhere.

I grew to love that station. It became, as East Dulwich Grove had before it, and Sestri Levante was to be after it, and Milan once was somewhere between, the starting point of escape, the funnel of my escapades, and a name synonymous with truancy. I enjoyed the desolation of the platform, the visual confirmation of my thoughts. And I enjoyed the sheer size of the Intercity train, throbbing towards that little outpost hacked out of the surrounding fields, visible for miles either way in the flatness of that landscape. Not least, I enjoyed the way my journey to it missed out entirely the hideous ribbon development that lined the road from the shrivelled grey metropolis of King's Lynn South.

The train brought whatever friends or family came to see me, and although it would then take them away again, I could at least follow.

Maybe my best day was when I boarded the four thirty-five at Liverpool Street in London and jostled and edged my way down the very crowded corridors until I found a place between two compartments to park myself and my little black suitcase. The commuters from Cambridge and Audley

End used this train, packing it with their pinstripes and their Scotches and waters and gins and tonics and packets of salted nuts. These commuters tend to know one another on a surname and 'What'll you have tonight?' basis only, and they somehow resent any form of travel other than city commuting, seeming to despise any passenger who doesn't work in the city and live either in Cambridge or Audley End. I'd had a bit of difficulty finding anywhere to wedge my miniature suitcase in the minefield of executive briefcases that took up most of the floor space of the train. Then the guard came along, and the train started to hightail its way through the slums of Hackney and the fallen splendour of Bethnal Green, and the guard, who knew my name from my many British Rail cheques due to the ticketless state of Magdalen Road, spoke to me. He said, 'Good evening,' and used all of my name, and then, as he moved by, he said quite loudly, 'I'll stop the train specially for you at Magdalen Road.' As he left, a flutter of whispers arose. 'Who is she? Who is she?' I stood, between a door and the lavatory, as proud as royalty to think that all those pinstripes thought that an Intercity express in 1983 was really going to be stopped, just for me.

But for all the fond moments, the rare hot summers, the heaped baskets of soft fruit, the roaring fires, it was the 'merciless iced east wind that knived me, and the blades of my own discontent'. The circumstances of my life seemed to have conspired with my own dreams and ambitions to produce in me a feeling of despair. My mother's slow death from cancer and my son's mismanaged birth had both played havoc with my strength and stability. Then, there was the not so sweet smell of success. I railed and raged against the concept of somehow having 'made it', got there. I felt that I was at the beginning of something very big, and the idea that I had somehow achieved all that I would or could in my life, and of my life being suddenly narrowed to one inessential sphere, truly disturbed me.

I had dreamed of Italy, and fantasised and remembered, many a time, but somehow I had never returned. Italy had become a kind of romantic touchstone for me. When my thoughts wandered, often as not they would visit the small footbridge over the Naviglio Grande in Porta Ticinese, Milan, where I had spent hours and hours of my adolescence staring down into the green water, watching it run with its cargo of bedsprings and packages and sodden litter of every kind. There was a plastic glove at the bottom of that canal which had caught in weeds and filled with water and which wafted eerily with a slow, underwater wave. At times, this smooth hand seemed to beckon. I thought, naïvely, that if I returned to Italy after that long passage of the years I would find happiness, as by some miracle, and all would be well. Instead, I found myself, and it was a self with which I could not sit happily.

My choice of location was fairly arbitrary: Sestri Levante, on the Riviera, was the one place where I was able to rent something big enough to house myself, my children, their nanny, my claustrophobia and my delusions of grandeur.

I had been working for six months on the screenplay of my novel, *The Slow Train to Milan*, and the film was due to be shot later that year. It was scheduled to take some three months in the filming, and I was to go out there for the whole time. When the shooting was postponed I decided to go anyway. It was to be my great adventure, the only one that I had actually tried to orchestrate.

I was so anxious for everything to be just right that at each stage of my journey I tried to shield myself from any initial disappointment. Thus I funked the train itself and flew out to Milan. I was travelling with my one-year-old son, and I felt that to re-travel the tracks after all those years with a small child might not be the ideal way to rediscover what had once been so essential to me. I asked the travel agent who sold me my air ticket what the nearest airport to Sestri Levante would be, and was told, only seconds later and with great authority, that Milan was the place. After hours of delay I arrived in Italy to find that the airport was an hour away from Milan, and then, later, that Sestri Levante was another five hours away by train and that there was no train for hours. By this time, however, I had brainwashed myself into seeing nothing but good and the promise of good, so I checked into the nearest big hotel with my bemused baby and spent the evening watching gibberish on the television, drinking brandy and musing on the wonders of the continent.

The next morning I walked, wheeling Alexander's pushchair through the maze of cars, towards Mussolini's massively decadent brainchild, across the wide car park of the Piazza di Savoia that separates the Hotel Bristol from Milan Central. I had to buy my ticket to Sestri Levante, and this I succeeded in doing, but only with extreme difficulty, confirming what I had begun to fear, that my grasp of the language (upon which I had counted) was virtually nil. I had hoped that the soap operas of the night before's television were in some strange, unintelligible language, and not Italian, since for fifteen years, when people asked me how many and which languages I spoke, I had always stood my Italian up to be counted, with some pride in my fluency. I had never once had to actually speak it again after my eighteenth birthday, but I felt (and remembered hearing) that one never forgot a language. It seemed I had.

I made my way back to the Hotel Bristol, unable, temporarily, to look up from the gutter at the stars and concentrating on giving myself a little pep talk on local colour. Okay, so I'd be unable to communicate with anything other than signs and smiles – at least the rest was there. The station itself, unchanged and immense with all its imperialistic paraphernalia, towering over the soldiers and conscripts and peasant women in black carrying their bundles.

And look, here was a gypsy woman, the very spirit of the South. There had been no gypsies at Wiggenhall St Mary the Virgin. I looked down into my son's ringlets as I considered all this, and my slightly dampened fire of enthusiasm for the Mediterranean and the castanets was rekindled. With my ticket to Sestri Levante in my handbag and my head full of Keats and Shelley, I wafted across the hundred yards that separated me from my hotel, mentally building up an Identikit picture of the warmth, ease and happiness that Italy, and particularly the Riviera, held in store for me.

Blinded by euphoria, I failed to see that the gypsy woman was cutting in towards me. Even after she had demanded money, I still failed to spot her obvious aggression, and mistook her dogged shouting to be her picturesquely brusque way of begging. My baby son was much quicker on the uptake than I was, and whimpered steadily as we watched the magpie turn into a crow, her fists and rags flapping threateningly around us.

All I needed to do was run to be clear of the maze of parked Fiats and Volkswagens and back on a streetful of people. Instead, however, I apologised profusely, as English people do so often when they have nothing to excuse and so rarely when they are genuinely in the wrong. I unzipped my handbag, mixing my volley of 'sorry's to her tirade of abuse. It was hard to undo, because she was already holding it for me and she was, I noticed, an unexpectedly powerful woman. Inside, I had expenses for six months in traveller's cheques and cash. I still cherished the notion of crossing this woman's palm with silver, even though silver in Italy comes down to coins so paltry that it would take a handful of them to buy a bubblegum. The stale garlic of her breath was very close to mine by the time I realised that she wasn't really a bubblegum person, and her wide palm was clenched tightly over my two thousand dollars in cash before I seriously wondered why she was nearly up to her elbow in my handbag.

As I stared in amazement, her arm slipped away, and I felt myself blush with embarrassment, thinking, 'She doesn't like me.' She had obviously seen me coming in the true sense of the phrase, but I don't think she had envisaged that I would be quite the easy touch that I was. Because the bag was around both my shoulder and my neck, there was some delay as she pulled her hand out of the mess of crunchy nut bars and Kleenex and dollars, and she momentarily lost her balance. This she steadied by resting her other large hand on my son Alexander's head. He screamed, and I came to my senses, and the gypsy and I began to arm-wrestle in the air. I gripped her forearm as though my very life depended on it, while she clawed at my arm with her long horny nails that seemed to be harbouring cultures of all the grime of Milan under them. Far from loosening my grip, my determination to hold on now, if need be to the death, was increased by the sight of the welts rising and the trickles of blood on my skin. I thought of tetanus jabs and the filth under her fingernails, and I thought of all the times I had given in in the past through my ever-constant desire to please, and as we dragged each other across the parking lot I remember thinking how I was dancing after all, after a fashion.

I suppose even gypsies get bored, and after a great deal of hissing and spitting and kicking and scratching, she began to let go. I had already resigned myself to a life-time of living with a withered arm and had decided that at least so would she. We were both too tired, when it came to the money, to pull it out of the other's hand, so most of it dropped on to the tarmac and some of it was torn in half.

As she reeled back from our tussle, the gypsy stood, a mass of tired muscle, against a backdrop of station wall. I hated her for having seen me as I was: a silly tourist, an incompetent fool. I watched her limp away, musing as to whether I had caused her limp, and hoping that I had. Then I picked up my scattered cash and calmed the incipient apoplexy in the pushchair and made my way back to the hotel, mournfully aware that the nation of Italy hadn't spread its red carpet, or even its cloak, for me, and that life wasn't necessarily going to be easy.

My trip from Milan to Genoa and thence to Sestri Levante was made in a mood of rare defiance. Every time anyone caught my eye, I dared them with my stare even to speak to me. Since it was an Italian train, and Italians on trains cannot resist speaking to everyone, even seething Englishwomen who glare, the full impact of my delayed rage was a little spoilt. I made up for this by practising, in my head, a speech of Shakespearian proportions to be addressed to the next middle-aged long-nailed gypsy I met. It was a curse, and I wished that I had cursed my attacker. By Pavia I had worked out all sorts of embellishments to this speech.

I could scarcely move my arm, it was so bruised and twisted. An hour into the journey, I found that the train had almost lulled away my rage. I began to feel sure that there must be a funny side to what had happened but I couldn't quite manage to see what it was. On the couple of occasions that I tried to smile, thus laughing off the whole incident, I found tears welling in my eyes. My fellow passengers interpreted this, together with my previous moroseness, as a sure sign that I had just been deserted in some way, and the word 'abbandonata' began to crop up as they discussed my affairs.

As the train approached Genova Principe I had a little talk with myself and decided that enough harm had been done without my dwelling further upon it. An elderly couple in the carriage had become inordinately fond of my son, so, feeling very sorry for myself, I made do with the fact that somebody liked him, me, us; and, virtually one-armed, and four hundred dollars down, I grudgingly watched the landscape as the train cut through mountains towards the baroque and decaying grandeur of Genoa.

The journey from Genoa to Sestri Levante takes an hour and is entirely made up of long tunnels and glimpses of the sea. These last seem to compete with each other for prettiness. The railway line is cut almost on the edge of the rock-face in places and the deep drops down into the turquoise water are studded with gnarled cypresses and silver-grey cinerarias that cling to the cracks in the stone. Away from the see-through Mediterranean sea, on the far side of the tracks, the mountains rise steeply into crests and valleys, and every few miles villages like contained landslides climb down from domed churches.

Since the train to Sestri was a *Locale*, it stopped all the way down the line at places like Portofino and Rapallo that were redolent with literary and other associations, and places like Zori and Zoagli that I'd never heard of. At each stop, schoolchildren and marketeers, workmen and nuns climbed on to the high train and then jostled down its corridors. Sitting huddled in my corner seat, the young Alexander asleep on my lap, I realised that what I remembered of Italy was its outward noise and inward calm, and its colour and my own sense of belonging there, but what I had forgotten was the reality of living there, and, worst of all, the language.

Alexander's vocabulary, at that stage, was limited to 'Bye bye train', 'Mamma', 'No', and 'Bye bye sea'. After years of silence, I had become a compulsive talker and a happy listener too. Whom would I communicate with now? Every time the train emerged from a tunnel, the sight of the sea filled me with a vague irrational hope, but every time it blacked into a tunnel, I brooded in the ensuing darkness on a life of monosyllables and slow dictionary phrases as the inane patter of constant repetition rang through my head with the same rhythm of the train: 'Bye bye sea'. Perhaps Alexander had inherited a touch of the family clairvoyance. Perhaps that was why all he ever said was his farewell to the water, because he knew and had foreseen this coming year of trains and tunnels that was to steal away so many times those fine views of the sea.

Had the train been going to Naples, I could have moved myself to tears labouring that theme. But Chiavari loomed up and was quickly passed without so much as a glimpse of its cathedral and with rather too ample views of its sprawling slums. Then it was Lavagna with its grey volcanic beach on the one side and its unseen but famous slate quarries out of sight on the other, and then a concrete tunnel slashed with daylight to the sea, and then the peninsula of Sestri itself came into view.

7

I wed me to an exiled lot and bear the absence of the world

I arrived at Sestri Levante in October 1984, and although I had scarcely enjoyed the journey I left the compartment with a pang of regret which I immediately stored in the place in my brain permanently reserved for future nostalgia, and realised that Italy was in fact working its old magic on me and that I was already weaving the myth of pleasures past to resavour in moments to come. Some months later, Alexander expanded his rather exclusive and limited vocabulary to let in the phrase, 'Life's not so bad'. The first time he said this to me as I slumped in woe at my table, reduced to despair by some trivial detail of my life, I realised just how many times I must have used the phrase myself in those first months in Italy.

What with my new battle scars and the perennial pushchair, I descended from the train with a little less elegance than I might have desired in what was to be my home town for over a year. I was to be met at the station with keys to my flat. This had all been arranged from London, and I had phoned through my exact time of arrival from Milan. The platform emptied, and no one came. I thought bitterly, 'Shall they return to beating of great bells/In wild train-loads?/A few, a few, too few for drums and yells/May creep back, silent, to village wells/Up half-known roads.'

In the ticket hall, I paced a square around the marble rectangle of its floor. The clock on the wall informed me at each turn that although the minutes were passing slowly, a lot of minutes were passing by. Propping my small suitcase beside a telephone box that I found myself incapable of using, I wandered around the hall reflecting that if the Israelites had been as inefficient as I they would never have made it into Egypt. Trains came and went behind me on the many platforms of the incongruously large station for such a surprisingly small town. Outside, one strange street led into another. Unknown territory. I had arranged to rendezvous at the station itself, so I didn't dare go away.

With my one battered hand hanging loosely, I pushed Alexander's wheeled chair around that hall over and over again, making – as I later discovered – a comical sight for the ticket collector who watched my ill-humour and my disappointment and my unsteady pushing of the chair with puzzled amusement. It was October and the tourist season was over. Sestri Levante was preparing to hibernate. With every marble square I crossed I shed another layer of my confidence. I became aware of the ticket man bowed in his glass booth, watching me as I waited. I felt my paranoia mount as the time passed and no key came. I was sad: I had finally got to Italy after all those years only to get off on the wrong foot. I had wanted to return to my 'home' of when I was seventeen and foolish, and I had done so only to find that I was much aged but none the wiser. I was so sad that day, sad with myself and with the world, but mostly with myself, that I didn't want anyone to see how sad I was lest I begin to cry. I didn't like the ticket man watching me in my sudden loneliness. I wanted to ask him if my seven trunks had arrived from London. I felt I wouldn't feel so lonely even there if I knew that my trunks and books and clothes and rugs and pictures were waiting for me, but I didn't dare stumble with misremembered words and risk being laughed at. I didn't know then that the ticket man was Enrico, who spoke seven languages and was a kind of Nostromo of the Rivieran Railways, the most capable organiser I've ever met, and one who had virtually made a vocation of helping people. It was Enrico who would salvage my flight to Sestri from potential disaster to an odyssey of trains, but I didn't know that either, so I just kept thinking about the Egyptians and my arm and chocolate, because chocolate is one of the keys to happiness, and I was waiting for a key.

In Norfolk, I had felt the burden of being a good person, a nice person. I had wanted to be wild and reckless. I wanted a great love, and I wanted to develop a mean and vicious streak. Waiting in the ticket office at Sestri Levante, I wasn't sure I'd chosen the best way to go about it. Time, it seemed, was running out. Joanna had died, and I had to stop being so sorry for myself. But when I thought about me, a lump in my throat formed so quickly I felt I was growing an enormous adam's apple.

Eventually I was met and taken to my flat. Whatever had been left of my Italian dream deflated on arrival. The description was the same, but the reality was so different that I found myself speechless with disappointment. The balconies all opened on to the Via Aurelia and the streams of noisy traffic rattled the seemingly endless rooms with their fifties décor. I decided to abandon nine-tenths of the apartment and live in two rooms.

Day one was my birthday, a red morning in which I explored the hairpin streets of the town. After years of fleeting encounters I had come now, prepared and even anxious, to dig deeply into the underclay of casual meetings. Dressed to kill, I announced myself as available to the world, ready at last to peel off the onion layers of myself. The only person in the least excited by my new spirit of truth and adventure was me. I couldn't even say 'Look, Ma!' I led the bemused figure of Alexander in a new starched sailor suit down the high street as though on a voyage of discovery. Alas, there was no America at the end of the road, and, despite all the previous findings of Columbus and his men, the world did appear to be flat and I felt in real danger of falling off it.

It hadn't been like this for Byron and Stendhal. I drank a coffee and a brandy while Alexander dismantled a piece of chocolate cake. The café was entirely empty but for three waiters who stood behind the counter and stared. There was no ambiguity in those stares, they were clearly unwelcoming, shading to a grudging indifference as they reached my son.

I was confident that I would win their hearts: I had merely come at the wrong time; I'd brazen it out. There was worse in the war, I told myself, as the image of the friendly Italy of my youth faded into the dregs of my drink. Years back, in

Bologna, I had known crews of old ladies with whom I had gossiped and sipped tea and discussed outmoded court circulars. Out in the bars, I had mixed with young intellectuals with minds whose temperature hovered permanently at a few degrees below spontaneous combustion. Then, I had known and charmed elderly lonely men into telling me their life-stories. I had around me what Joanna used to call the second eleven, a team of young men who were ready and willing and standing by for such time as I should deign to call them into play. I had also lived at the centre of a group of devoted friends. When I felt lonely in Bologna or Milan in my teenage days, it was because I chose to, from within my tapestry of fans and would-be lovers. Now, fourteen years on, I was no longer sixteen and looking twelve and the swaddle of kindness that falls automatically over children in Italy was rudely denied me. Alexander was offered a corner of it, but he was too shy to take it.

Looking back, I realise that my presence there, unannounced and unexplained, must have seemed more sinister and threatening to them than their silence and hostility did to me. I was invading their privacy, while they were merely squashing my dreams. The season was over and the fifty thousand summer-timers had shrunk back to the twenty-five thousand locals who were all busy improving their homes and their children. The last bars closed at nine, the restaurants rarely opened, and the cafés were almost permanently empty. Sestri Levante didn't hibernate in winter; it died.

I made an extensive search of the village and became convinced that what Byron and Ruskin had said about its purple skies was a touch over the top. And although Hans Christian Andersen had named one of the two facing bays 'The Bay of Fairytales', it was a bay around which fairytales could be woven, rather than a watery tombola out of which they could be fished. But the other bay, 'The Bay of Silence', truly was just that. Looking down on it from the cypress and acacia copse that overhung the high track above it, I found myself speechless with admiration and pleasure at the stillness and calm that emanated from its waters.

This contrasted sharply with the rather hostile stillness of the town. Enrico later told me that in Genovese dialect the outlying villages called Sestri Levante the two-faced place, because of the nature of its landscape and the fickle, double-edged character of its people. Everywhere, and nearly every one of the Sestresi – so he assured me – had these two faces. For one riven by my own schizoid fears, it seemed an unfortunate place to be.

It began to rain. I needed a nanny. I had never reared a child on my own, nor lived in such solitary confinement. In my dream, I had envisaged a wonderfully keen, efficient and jolly local housekeeper who would be easy to find and a joy to be with. This person failed to materialise. Even the diluted version of her – a girl to help out and live in – was impossible. It seemed that girls didn't live in, and if they did, then not as nannies. So I was trapped; slowly I would mummify in my flat with its corridor as long as a hospital's and its dark rooms leading off it like fishbones from a central spine.

I knew nobody there. I was starting from scratch in a place that had put a formica veneer to protect its core from the inane scratches of the likes of myself. I would live in a Bay of Silence.

It was Enrico, who came from another country, twenty minutes away along the track, who initiated me into the mysteries of the silence. The gist of his teachings seemed to imply that no one would talk to me for about a year, and then, if I was really really nice and stayed right through a summer, they might. It was October, and I had come for six months. But between reclaiming my trunks and unpacking the first of them for three appalled Customs officials, who watched the unravellings of my belongings – stuffed birds, nappies, prints, books, Victorian gowns, and a miscellany of objects that they couldn't even identify, let alone name and write out in duplicate for their declarations – I grew daily fonder of that harsh, inhospitable town. The Customs men eyed my stack of luggage with obvious alarm, and with their sights set firmly on their suppers they finished off my long document of imported goods with an italic etcetera.

Sestri Levanti itself I wooed and won like a lover, with great difficulty and guile. I loved it with a devotion born out of rejection. With a perverse obstinacy, I set out to win the town that had ignored me. It was, in its way, a delicate operation, and I began with its heart, the station, getting to know the men who worked there, and their shifts and offices, before getting to know the hangers-on, the tramps and the drunks and the pushers. Then I learned the timetable, the principal trains, *Espressi*, *Diretti*, *Locali* and *Merce*. Having thus established a base, I shunted up and down the track, certain of a friendly face on my return, and a smile and even a cup of coffee or a glass of wine. I was able to carry out this strategy thanks to the assistance of Enrico, who was master of all trades and jack of none. Without the hundreds of minutes snatched between his shifts when he coaxed and encouraged me in the lore and language of Liguria, my mini-invasion of the Riviera – which is what my subsequent visits have come to be – would have come to nought.

Every twenty minutes a train went through the station. At nine o'clock the Naples Express passed through from Boulogne, and at nine thirty the *Dirette* to Florence, and at twelve thirty-five the Rome Express stopped there. Alexander showed unpromisingly little interest in this timetable, but I was past needing encouragement by then. Soon, I told myself, I would be on all those trains; soon my breath would linger in every tunnel between there and Sicily.

Meanwhile, what the population of Sestri denied me, the geography supplied. The twin beaches curved around their respective bays, one with its black sand and the other with its fair sand and seaweed and pigeons picking over it. There were palm trees on the esplanade. I hadn't expected palm trees, and they came as a great bonus in the dipping scales of my contentment. Whatever hopes I had I jettisoned to the sea, and whatever plans I made I concentrated around the trains and the tracks and the station building itself with its long stretch of yellow ochre and its shifts of friendly faces.

One day my Italian returned, not bit by bit, but in a rush. I was trying to rent a television set, and the owner thought that I was trying to buy it, and a terrific disagreement ensued about the price. I despaired of getting through, but I desperately wanted the television. My flat was silent every night, and I wanted to hear voices, even if they were the voices of Cagney and Lacey dubbed into Italian under the title of *New York*. I became incoherent with desire; I prayed to the god of soap operas to let me have this set, and suddenly I was visited by the gift of tongues, and was able to tell the dealer exactly what I wanted from him, which was exactly what I got, a big black and white television set with an inside aerial and a table to stand on to be fitted with the right voltage plug by him right away. After the job was done, and Quincy was flitting across the screen rolling his rrrs to the dubbing process, the television dealer shrugged and said, in Italian, 'But why didn't you say what you wanted from the start?' After he left, I felt that a small flag could be planted outside the door of his shop to show that, however slowly, I was luring the locals out of their monastic cult. I had proved myself to be human and no known relation of the she devil. The television dealer had a daughter who had been to Battersea. Did I know Battersea?

'Oh, yes, the power station.'

'Exactly.'

I was the right sort after all, or would be, if Enrico was right, after a year with a summer.

I wanted to go dancing. I wanted to see bright lights and hear the excitement in people's voices as they drank and talked in cafés that stayed open all night. The nearest I got to this was the red-light zone, a strip of thirty yards of road at the mouth of the tunnel that linked Sestri to Lavagna. Sometimes, when I was feeling tired and emotional, I'd wander up to the hookers' patch and watch their camaraderie and their banter. There was a layby in which the bulk of their business was performed on the back seats of cars, mostly Fiats and Volkswagen Golfs. I used to lean against the low stone wall that dropped down to the sea and envy the prostitutes their very identity. They knew who they were and had a place, however superficially squalid, in society; and they were obviously friends with each other and could laugh at their predicament, plying their trade as they did in the pouring rain. I looked at them and mused that they had their short skirts and their cigarettes and jokes as they crossed the road like gathering martins, while I had only the indestructible pushchair and a gorge of self-pity and Alexander who had not yet learned to tell me that life wasn't so bad.

Nobody respectable from the town crossed the invisible line that divided the esplanade from the trauma of ill repute. A number of people did come along that road, though, to a point some way further on where an ancient underpass doubled back towards the station and the other side of town. Many of these passers-by were very aged, and they reminded me in their shrouded macs of the old crones in the fairytales who could grant wishes to silly wanderers like me. It amused me to think, as I watched the friendships of the mostly fat, middle-aged prostitutes with their mascara running in the rain, that a kindly hag might mistake my wish for company for a desire to join that group professionally, and wave a knotted wand that would turn me into seventy-five kilos of stale merchandise against my will. Even I had to admit though, that if there was a ladder of good beats and bad, then the tunnel's mouth at Sestri would have to rate very low on it, and that if, in certain circles, prostitution could seem glamorous, there was certainly no glamour on that wet bit of road.

The idea of illicit sex, of courtesans, Nell Gwyns and Mrs Keppels, Harriette Wilson herself, and the young girls of Montmartre, used to fascinate me as a child. I thought it would be very romantic to be a French prostitute at the turn of the century, mixing in Paris with painters I loved and admired. I even bought a long tight skirt so that I could learn to mince as I walked, and steel-capped stilettos that clicked and scraped. It didn't take me long to understand that not all the girls would get Modigliani and most of them would get the clap, so I turned my ambitions to poetry, at the age of twelve, and have never really regretted it. Yet now there was something about the brightness of their clothes and the thickness of their lipstick that drew me back day after day to glean some kind of colour from the Mediterranean and the driving, relentless rain. I suppose I was missing the garish flair of the gypsies, now that my heart was temporarily hardened to their tribe.

In Venezuela and in Norfolk I had wondered if I would ever return to Italy, and I feared that if I did, everything would be changed, and the old magic of the slow train to Milan would have gone for ever. I suppose one is often inclined to believe that the people and the things that one loves disappear as soon as one loses interest in them. Not surprisingly, the Italian railway system had survived without me, and although the years that had passed between us had seemed deeply significant for me, certain of the trains appeared to be the very ones that I had known and loved before. I worried once that the worn tartan of the seats of 1970 would have become plastic, and that the cardboard rolls would be kept as soft as cotton wool in cling-film wrappers. But in 1984 there were still trains that looked as though they might have been running in 1894. There were trains with wood-panelled interiors and tiny, narrow, wooden-slatted seats. These were the sort that often chugged down the Riviera, the sort that Jesse James might have leant out of and not looked out of place. There were also double-decker trains and computerised tickets, but, basically, nothing had changed.

I have always been drawn to places and things where people seem to fit in naturally, the kind of environment where people don't look out of place. And hence, somewhere for me, too, to belong. It is often easier, for anyone born of two or more nationalities, or even classes, to 'belong' abroad, away from home, than wherever 'home' is meant to be. There is no guilt attached to feeling different when one is a mere tourist, and there is a vast amount of pleasure to be gained from adapting to an alien society, and then – the ultimate goal – being accepted by it. To pass undetected in a foreign country is an honour. To pass undetected in one's native country is a slight.

In Sestri Levante, I didn't exactly pass unnoticed; I was just ignored. After many weeks of soul-searching and closet-weeping and re-reading Byron's letters, I decided to accept the silence as a challenge. I had tried pacing the high street and the esplanade thinking defiantly, 'You wouldn't be like this to Byron,' and, frankly, it worked, because after wearing out a couple of pairs of stilettos on the cobbles I realised a very profound truth. It seems simple now, and obvious, but it was hard work at the time and involved the shattering of a lifelong fantasy: I wasn't Byron, or even Stendhal or Shelley, nor even Mary Shelley. It saddened me then, and left me with the vanity (and the appetite) of a caterpillar.

I looked at my reflection in shop windows as I passed them by, and all I saw was my own face, bereft, for once, of the aura of wit and brilliance that I'd borrowed from the poets and heroines of the past all my life.

The next five months of my life were to be lived on trains, criss-crossing Italy from Sestri Levante to Brindisi, and back and forth, covering thousands and thousands of miles of track along which I shed thousands of delusions and reinvented hundreds of illusions. My life was a mish-mash of the insides of compartments and corridors and platforms, my friends were the transitory friendships of long journeys and my loves were the volatile loves where passion is quickened by the hourglass it can run through.

Sometimes I branched across to Naples or down to Cosenza, but mostly I followed a route from Brindisi to Sestri Levante via Bologna. I had never been so manic or so free. My children were cared for, and my house was not my house, and there were no animals or trees or sad, needful people leaning on me. I had finally escaped all my responsibilities, only to find that my new weightlessness could actually smother me. I need the intrigue and the sense of power from unravelling other people's lives. That my own life was not a happy one, I realised, was quite unconnected with my intense involvement in other people's lives. The train to Brindisi gave me a sense of security and, after the first few months, of truly belonging. Here was time and people, time and place, and even a fairly accurate timetable to go with it.

Winter came, and snowed heavily on the Riviera for the first time in sixty years, and I didn't like it. All through it, I trekked back and forth from Brindisi to Bologna, missing the dead Italophiles of a bygone era. I scrabbled around in my own brain, so rudely and recently stripped of its Byronic trappings, and I didn't like that either. What was life without my heroes? What was left without my dream? During the dull spells on the train, after Pescara, edging through the night and the Abruzzi with all the coffee and the chocolate and the conversation spent, I pondered my discovery, and decided that the blame lay in my early reading. In times of trouble a scapegoat often helps a quick recovery. The scapegoat is frequently oneself. This time, I felt reluctant to blame myself, and very keen to believe that no child should read too many novels or romantic biographies before the age of five, lest, like ducks, they imprint the subjects of those books on to themselves.

Out of the confusion I drew comfort from my travelling companions, the routine of the timetable, and, later, the splendour of the almond blossom that turned the bare, southern fields into cascades of variegated pinks.

By January, I had the protection of Rita, a slimmer and younger version of my ideal housekeeper. She had a family of her own, and a house where I took daily asylum. My daughter had come for a month and gone, leaving a host of young men on scooters asking after her. The railway rides kept me stable, and the constant stream of people whom I met on them gradually defrosted my rather mad delusions. Each time I spoke to someone new I would explain that I was a novelist, and they all seemed somehow glad at this. It served to remind me that, nominally, that was what I was, and I began to write *The Bay of Silence*. In it, I forced my characters to cope with and exorcise my fears. By the end of March, I had finished, and there were signs of spring everywhere. My six months were nearly up, the term of my escape was nearly over, but I decided to stay in Italy and make my home there, and come to know it as it really is, and not as I had wished to shoehorn it into being. I also decided that I liked being on the move so much that I would never again even try to live anywhere all the time. I would commute across Europe, by train, between England where my family and work were based, and Italy where my heart was grafting. Every time I went down to the sea, to stand on the narrow beach of the Bay of Silence, I felt the waves lapping at my feet like a watery communion. Perhaps that was the nearest I would ever come to feeling religious.

Three narrow passageways join the high street to that beach. Each one of them is encrusted with sandy ropes and half-buried chains where the fishing boats lie between catches. Dozens of cats live and sleep in these boats, secure in their knowledge that the fishermen will feed them on scraps and heads and guts. Italian cats, like good Italians, eat lots of pasta. Old ladies put out little bits of paper with piles of left-over spaghetti and lasagne on their doorsteps all over town. But there were more cats on the beach than anywhere else. After hours of scouring the sand for sea glass, I'd return to my flat or go to Rita's with my haul of smooth, coloured chips of glass, from the bay to the town through one of the alleyways. Back on the street, girls with Benetton jackets and Gucci shoes and unfriendly stares seemed to be thinking, 'Just who does she think she is?' Where once, months before, this had unnerved me, it now re-echoed in my head: just who did I think I was? I still didn't really know, but what with the spring in the air, there were distinct possibilities of my caterpillar self becoming a butterfly in the not too distant future, and meanwhile, I was the mother of Alessandro and the child Iseult.

Off the rails

Engine of panic
On a runaway train,
Cut cord of my travels
Unravelling like spilt
Bile in the carriage.
Years of bitterness
Erupting down the line.

And there were no
Stations,
No places to hide or genuflect,

85

OFF THE RAILS

No one to measure the miles,
Nothing to feel
But the tunnel
Cut through the rocks.

Mud on my hands
And time to steal,
Darkness to smell,
And always my own sick smile
Funnelled on to strange faces,
Last vestige of the mask
After it cracked.

I broke my head and made
A jigsaw puzzle
For a while;
So many pieces,
So many places,
And still no stations
Even though I've put them back.

Nowhere to go
But on down the stark track.

8

Lost in Corfu

With the unfurling of the oleander leaves and the budding of sweet chestnuts, I jettisoned the dregs of my Byronic dreams, casting them into the Ligurian sea. It was February and cold, and I had finally abandoned romance for practicality. Then two things happened. The first was a visit to Rome where I went to the Byron, Keats and Shelley museum housed in the flat by the Spanish Steps where Keats died of consumption.

I thought, wrongly, that my recent stumbling would have made me immune to my old heroes, as one grows immune to the entreaties of former lovers. I flicked through discoloured diaries, manuscripts, prints and letters of veiled eroticism with feigned uninterest, and then, immediately, set sail for Greece.

The other incident seemed unimportant, initially, but was in fact to be the turning point of my future years. I had moved from my private vanity into a more public light when my first book went into print. A consequence of this was an ever-expanding sequence of photographs of me, which varied from the unflattering to the frankly ghastly. There were shots, clicked by many a skilled hand, that gave me a face that could have hastened Dracula back into his coffin. The dark rings under my eyes joined to meet the rising shadows from my neck, and my eyes themselves often seemed drugged, or else bored half to death. My nose (a wonderful inheritance from my mother) can look very strange at the wrong angle, and most cameras seemed to stand stubbornly at the wrong angle to that ancestral feature. So it was decided, *chez* MacBeth, from the muddy depths and flats of Norfolk, that a painting should be made of me to rectify the photographic injustices of my recent publicity.

The search for the perfect painter began in 1982. The

National Portrait Gallery in Trafalgar Square seemed a fine place to start, so George and I went to the annual portrait exhibition there. Much of the exhibition seemed to be a sublimation of the kitchen sink, a subject, perhaps because I have spent so many hours of my life drudging at one, I have never found particularly to my taste. However, not all rain is acid, even in Trafalgar Square, and we came to a good corner where we were both struck by a picture called 'Un soleil de l'amour'. This was a portrait of a young man prostrate on a chaise-longue. He drapes, numb, at the eye of the hurricane, entombed by the symbolism of love and a broken love affair, redolent both of suicide and of the crucifixion with all its undertones of betrayal.

We noted the name of the painter, Duff-Scott, and George wrote to him, care of the gallery, to commission a portrait. I remembered, to the right of that picture, a jacket and hat lying like a headless figure, a ghostly John the Baptist into which I already imagined my hitherto headless image taking shape. Duff-Scott, however, wrote back to George, in wonderful italic script, that he regretted he did not wish to paint his wife. The name receded, and although I too felt regret, my nose grew no more and life continued on its circular timetable.

Two years later and months after I had left Norfolk for Italy, another beautiful letter arrived. Duff-Scott wanted to paint a sad Magdalen and had seen my picture in a magazine. He had not, he explained, made the connection between George and myself because of the myriad different surnames that we used. Would I now sit for him, if he, in thanks, gave me the painting when it was done? Flattery is like the Rome Express, it takes my breath away and wins my heart. The letter was forwarded to me in Sestri Levante, and all that icy February I carried it with me, fraying at the much opened creases like a talisman that would one day lead me back into myself.

I carried it with me as I set out for Greece, and three days later it was still warm in my pocket as I returned. There was no time to make a longer visit. I had forgotten, when I boarded the night ferry at Brindisi, that I was actually on my way back to Sestri, where I had a small shy child to collect.

I fell in love with Corfu. Not exactly at first sight because my circumstances at the time were more demanding of any attention than was the port before me. I had sailed in a big antiquated ferry that was churning its way from island to island and then to Piraeus itself. There were only a few people travelling that night, and most of them were lorry-drivers on their way to Athens, or American tourists temporarily immobilised by the straitjackets of their immense backpacks. Together with a dearth of shampoo and a penchant for fizzy drinks, these transatlantic travellers were all on the same circuit. Like battered hats and boots on a Monopoly board, they travelled round and round, stopping at different places on the board as they 'did' Europe. They were the last stragglers of the old Grand Tour, seeing as many places as they could before settling down to a future of real estate and responsibilities.

Because they had all been to, or were going to, the same places, they had a common vocabulary that joined them in instant, if ephemeral, friendships. Their presence on the ferry made the boat itself seem like a massive corridor on a trans-Europe train, the noise of engines and distant murmurings peppered only by coded conversations consisting almost entirely of place names as they re-created their travels by swapping cities and extended monosyllabic exclamations. There seemed always to be more common places, dozens and dozens of them, enough to last the entire night. Enough to last the three days to Athens – enough, probably, to last the next sixty years of evenings in Pittsburgh, Ohio, or Plainfield, New Jersey.

I was tired. I'd been in stations and trains all the previous night, and bar-crawling through semi-silent bars all day. After what seemed like hours, the litany of towns stopped abruptly as a girl leaned across into her canvas money-belt and asked, 'Where are you heading?'

I told her I didn't know.

'We're all going to Athens – everyone is going to Athens.'

The hidden Bolshevik in me rose up then, and made its exit. I woke up the purser, who was irritated to have his sleep disturbed, but willing to forgive me if I shared his cabin. I explained that I wanted to get out at Corfu, the first potential stop on the itinerary. He showed me the merits of his cabin – a photograph of his mother, a bottle of wine, the grime of his unchanged underpants – and eventually he took my word for it that I didn't want to see any more of him than that, and that I did want to disembark at seven the next morning.

I had no cabin of my own, so I wandered back down the plywood gangway to the bar and deck. The purser followed me. I quickened my step, thinking that he had come to tell me yet again that any prospective liaison between us need only be for one night. (He seemed to think that this would suddenly heighten his attractiveness to me, for he had repeated it several times in broken English.) Instead, he said, 'You have my cabin, I go with friend, you sleep, I no trouble, I go.'

Then he led me back to his cabin and left me there. Although it sounded to me like the oldest trick in the book, I was desperately tired, and I took advantage of his absence to sleep a deep and restorative sleep in his low bunk in the grimy cabin which smelt of incense and stale wine and sweat. I first barricaded the door in such a way that, if he did return, he would have to break all his possessions to get back into the cabin. However, his offer was quite genuine and the only sound to disturb me was the rumble of the engines. Next morning, at dawn, he escorted me to the disembarkation point. I thanked him for his bunk.

'Ah,' he sighed, stroking his groin sadly, 'you like the bed, but you miss the champion.' As he finished this sentence, he waved what appeared to be a small but perfectly formed erection at me.

I looked as politely noncommittal as I could.

'You never make jig-a-jig with Greek man?' he demanded suddenly.

'No,' I whispered, following him still through the bowels of the ship, past steel gangways and green-painted, half-rusted stairs and boilers.

'Is for that,' he told me, satisfied now that there was nothing personal.

Half-way down a narrow stairway to the lorry deck, the miniature, fat purser swivelled round, and seemed to have got himself stuck on the narrow girth of the stair.

'Fat,' he said, struggling to free some of his own from the rusty embrace of the wall and rail beside him. 'Fat don't mean nothing, and this,' he pointed to his balding grease pate, 'and this,' he jabbed towards his obligingly wide open mouth which was half emptied of teeth, and looked about as unappetising as any I'd seen but appeared to have very lively tonsils, 'they are nothing,' he continued, but not downstairs because he still had bits of himself wedged into the railings.

'Love,' he announced, 'love matters. Only a Greek man know how to love.'

The ferry lurched violently and then shuddered back as it docked. The purser was flung unceremoniously down the remainder of the stairs, landing in a position that made him seem even less of an Ionian Casanova than he had done before in his string vest. He was hurrying now, past huge parked lorries. The wide door of the lorry deck was lowered noisily to form a gang-plank. Behind was the captain in starched new whites, the crumpled but undeterred purser, two sailors in regulation jumpers and me, alone with a tiny black leather suitcase.

The winding gear completed its task, and the gang-plank touched the dock. I walked tentatively, clicking my stilettos on the metal floor, across the twelve-foot bridge they had made for me, leaving their amused voices behind as I teetered towards what appeared to be a deserted port.

There was grey mist, grey concrete and grey metal everywhere. In half an hour from that no man's land annexed to the Greek Customs and Excise was the town of Corfu itself and the island behind it. In half an hour I would be drinking thin Nescafé with condensed milk, bread and eggs and strawberry jam.

As the bus rattled into the nowhere of inland Corfu, I felt something stirring in my blood that had lain sluggishly for months, or even years. I felt the beginnings of a new life rising out of the clinker of my old one, and something about the island and its magical beauty was at the core of it. It is, I am sure, very convenient, if one is going to be foolish and rash, to be a novelist. The continual weaving of stories and life-styles enables the weaver endlessly to escape and begin again, and then, with skilful plotting, to make the new beginnings seem like part of a grand plan. So now I conjured up a new image of the Mad Bad Lord and refrigerated, metaphorically, a large part of my heart until such time as I should discover his reincarnation, or someone very like him, while my dreams began to get very involved with the idea of Corfu and the Adriatic, with mainland Greece, out of view but on the horizon, and Turkey far beyond it.

I had arrived in Corfu with a childlike view of the island, believing that it was enough to land and stand somewhere and know it, as one might a sandcastle or an unlit bonfire. The very notion that there was an inland to get lost in seemed strange. And yet, within an hour of quitting the city, I was in a village so small that I kept leaving it in my attempts to get my bearings. I had also come to believe, not without some measure of success, that I had the biblical 'gift of tongues'. I spoke good Spanish, French and Italian, passable German and Portuguese. I had once spoken reasonable Dutch and Russian, and upon hearing numerous other languages I had found it possible to follow the drift of what people were saying without needing to have recourse to a phrase book or interpreter. Alas, the Greek language proved to be the proverbial Greek to me. It used to be said that if one spoke English clearly and loudly enough, anyone could understand it, whether they came from France or Fiji, Cairo or the Kalahari desert. The people I met in this village, whose name I would record now if I knew it, seemed to feel the same way about Greek. Apparently quite thrilled by my presence, and eager to talk, they spoke to me continually, taking the raising of my arms and shaking of my head as an encouragement to speak louder and louder. Some of the older women seemed to be particularly entranced by my stiletto heels, which became the object of many questions and much laughter. After a great deal of feeling and cloth-rubbing it looked as though they wanted me to display them on a wire fence. No one showed any signs of understanding my appeals for a bus stop, road sign or bar.

I was hungry and confused. After moving my hand repeatedly towards my mouth, and chomping with a satisfied smile, the group, which consisted mostly of bowed elderly women, was none the wiser. Two of them had donkeys tethered to a fence, and I went over to one of these and, pulling up a handful of grass, made as though to eat it. A look of almost imperceptible concern flitted across a couple of faces, so I held the grass to one of the donkeys, which ate it. I was reminded of the Boxing Day parties of my youth when everyone in the family would be tired and liverish, and the supposed jollity of Christmas had proved to be transparent, but could not be admitted to be so, and games like charades and 'in the manner of the word' were concocted for unenthusiastic players. This was my charade, and I was acting it so badly, I felt, that no one would ever guess, and I would be shamed in front of everyone. The owner of the munching donkey caught the look of disappointment on my face and handed me the leather rein of her donkey to hold. I refused; she insisted; I refused; and within seconds I was holding the damp stained reins in my hand. Every time I tried to put them down, a flurry of anxious fingers again closed my own around the bits of worn leather.

Somewhere in the distance, a church bell tolled. I thought I must have been the only person to hear it, since no one else seemed to have done so, or to have heard of time at all. There was no sign of anyone knowing that the twentieth century had arrived and was more than three-quarters through. In fact, they showed no signs by their dress and baskets, tools and mules and donkeys, that the Renaissance had come and gone and was keenly reawaited.

What had been a crisp, sunny day chilled into a winter evening. Standing at the small crossroads with unmade tracks leading off in four winding directions, with the stone cottages of the hamlet huddled together behind us and nothing but thousands (possibly millions) of immense and ancient olive trees for as far as the eye could see, I knew that I was lost.

I had chosen this village rather than another because many of the black-clad people on the bus got off there too. While the heap of enormous baskets and paniers and bundles were unloaded by a team effort at the front of the vehicle, I sat near the back, hemmed into my window seat by an old man with watery eyes who had been sitting grimly beside me chewing imaginary water ever since the first stop after Corfu town. As the last of the baskets were being handed down, he shuffled to his feet and began the elaborate process of walking down the littered aisle of the bus to the door. Long before he reached it, I decided to get off there too, rather than risk a less populous area further on. There was something reassuring about the gabble of voices, the animated shoving and heaving of the wicker loads into place and the general excitement that the other passengers had of having arrived. The old bus teetered into the skyline and disappeared from sight. As it left, I half noticed that there didn't seem to be a corresponding stop on the other side of the road for a bus to return by. But I also thought, half jokingly, that there could scarcely be an enormous bus dump out on the middle of the island where battered buses went to rest after wending their way inland, never to return.

Everywhere I looked, there were olive groves the likes of which I had never seen. In Liguria there are olive trees, whole hillsides of them terraced there since Roman times, but they bore only a passing resemblance to the massive black trunks of these Greek plantations. The grey-blue green of the leaves was the same, and the silvery hue from afar that was like a sheen, and the smell and feel of the bark was the same, but where the trees in Italy grew gnarled and contorted, but only to a certain height and only to a given size despite their one or two centuries of age, the olive groves of Corfu were more like holm oaks in their size, and the girth of the trunks were of Amazonian proportions.

On leaving the bus, most of the locals shouldered their bundles, ducked into the nearest grove, and disappeared into its dense foliage. Thinking that something rather special must lie beyond these trees, I followed them. From the very first, the other passengers had become invisible to me, lost in the primeval wood, but I heard their voices somewhere ahead, calling and laughing to each other. After much unseemly scrambling, and digging my stilettos out of swampy grass, I came to a small road. There was no one in sight. I walked a little along the unmended surface and then decided to return to the village I had first descended at, because there was no sign of human habitation anywhere. To this end, I went back into the olive grove above me and wandered for what seemed like hours, confused by the trees themselves. The contortions of their trunks was such that each tree seemed individually recognisable, and I used them as landmarks to guide me through the wood. Where on my way down I had seemed merely to flounder through a terrace built between two roads and to have negotiated its undergrowth with relative ease, I now found myself tackling what appeared to be an entire hill slope, with only a little daylight filtering through the green veil of the upper leaves. Even the undulations of the terrain had changed, now: up no longer took me automatically back to the upper road, nor down out on to the lower one.

A panic of the Brothers Grimm type took hold of me, and the drifting music of voices that had first lured me into the wood disappeared in a fear of the grasping branches and the tripping ferns underfoot. The old tales of wolves and bandits filled my head. The trees were wonderful, but sinister too. I wanted now just to admire them from the outside and not find myself flung from one to the next in my efforts to extricate myself from the cat's cradle of their boughs. When I finally saw a fringe of daylight I threw myself at it, sobbing and panting, and emerged on to the dirt track that led to the hamlet where I was to spend the rest of the afternoon. It could not have been more welcome a sight. And if I lingered longer than I wanted, it was because the sheer relief at seeing people and dwellings again and enough, at first, to keep me there. My having disentangled myself from an olive grove was not, I knew, the kind of intrepid feat that Livingstone or Amundsen might boast of, but I was content to bask in the daylight, which was kind enough to be sunlight, and congratulate myself on not having been reduced to spending the night under the damp trees whimpering for the morning.

There was a distinct dampness in the air, rising, no doubt, from the waterlogged turf all around us. I turned the black velvet collar of my short jacket up around my neck and nestled a little into it. The mimes and the mumblings had all been in vain, yet that one gesture of my collar could not have produced more results had it been one of d'Annunzio's finest orations to the assembled company in their local dialect.

The donkey, which was still nominally in my charge, was taken from me and yanked down the road, while, simultaneously, the entire group scattered, some back to the hamlet, and others in the wake of the donkey and its mistress. A hand, as gnarled and twisted as the olive trunks themselves took hold of mine and pulled in that direction. Every joint was misshapen by rheumatism, and the knuckles had swollen long ago, the swellings seeming to have welded themselves to either side of the fingers. Most of the women I came across inland on Corfu had misshapen hands, and their backs were stooped and bent in degrees directly relating to their age, so that the oldest were nearly bent double and quite unable to straighten up. The dampness of the island and the months of olive-picking, all done manually, had started this; and the days spent turning the great Roman wheels of the presses completed the process.

All through the hours spent at the crossroad, finches of every description had come and gone, scattering the air with their birdsong. As our procession made its way downhill, a flock of assorted birds darted and followed overhead, settling now and then on the almond blossom whose white petals sweetened the air. At an unmarked point on the track the donkey turned right and everyone followed. The grasp of my hand by the bony knotted fingers that held it was so tight that I could not have pulled myself free, but it was also so ruthlessly friendly now that I didn't want to.

A pile of stones marked the entrance to a homestead. On closer inspection the pile turned out to be a shed in which iron tools, worthy of the iron age, were stacked. Beyond it was another stone construction which, again, looked little more than a haphazard arrangement of rough boulders.

Inside it was a house with several rooms running backwards off the first. In the far corner of this room, and merging into the natural shadows, a really old woman was sitting by a wood hearth, cooking something in a pot and poking at the ashes. She was so doubled that it seemed doubtful that she could stand at all. Dressed all in black as most of the women were, only the wizened lines of her face showed by the embers. Nobody addressed the old woman; she might have been deaf, or just half dead, it was hard to tell. With imperceptible movements of her draped spidery arms she began to shuffle hotplates on her open stove.

Soon the table was set with food and wine, and half-way through my meal, which they refused to share in any way other than by sitting or standing over me and talking fast and loud, a man emerged from the far end of the kitchen and came scowling into the room. He was dressed in a loose pair of trousers tied round with rope that could have been sewn from old sacks, and he wore a string vest and no shirt and he showed every sign of having just woken up. He spoke harshly to the women, who were miraculously silent, nodding only in my direction. His gruff manner disappeared and he came towards me, talking fast and smiling widely. Out of the greasy smoked wall behind me, he unearthed a shuttered window and opened it, throwing the room into a relative dazzle of twilight. He sat down opposite me, called out, was handed a glass, served more wine, and within minutes he proved himself to be a man of the world – that is, of the world beyond the olive grove and the stone hearth.

He spoke Italian, with the refined educated cadence of Tuscany, and seemed almost childishly pleased to practise it. Nothing could have been more different from the mono-syllabic grunts that he made periodically to his hushed womenfolk than his elaborate Florentine voice as he spoke to me. When first I had tried him with English and French and German, he had stared at me with a sullen incomprehension that robbed his face of his smile, yet at the cue of 'Italiano' he had seemed physically to ease himself into another persona.

First of all I explained how I came to be in his neighbourhood and how very much, with all due respect, I

97

would like to get out of it. He came from a large family, he told me – and I was reminded of Venezuela and the many cousins – among whom was a brother who would drive me back to Corfu town, and another who would chaperone me. (This last, not for my honour, but for that of his brother.) He also had a nephew in another village only some kilometres away who had a house to rent, and a sister who would like to cook for me. I tried to explain that I had to return to Italy to collect my son. He had a niece who loved children. I must go back to Italy, he insisted, and return; God had guided me to this village. I must come back with my son, right away. He jumped up from the table and began to order the women about. I quickly finished my meal, not knowing if I too would have to jump up and move into action on this new plan for my new house; I still had an enormous bowl of dried figs and almonds to munch through.

However, like an aging Action Man, he jumped back on to his bench and continued his courtly discussion. I was intrigued by his speech, and asked him where he had learned such Italian.

'Here,' he said, 'in this house, during the war.'

'But how?' I asked.

And he explained.

'The Italians came to Corfu with the Germans. We didn't like them, not the Germans, but especially not their puppet soldiers. Every week they came, requisitioning food, every week they took the things that it takes us all year to grow and make. First it was just a little, then more and more and always more. They were like the old olive press, taking the last drops of oil hiding in the skins of the olive.

'People talked, my brother, another, they told me how it was in Corfu town with the Italians always making trouble out of nothing, making life difficult for the peasants, for everyone, for themselves. And then, every week, they came to wring more food from us. First it was for the garrison, then for the garrisons in Italy, then it was for everyone, the Germans, the Italians, the families of the Italians, suddenly they all wanted my oil, my cheese, my figs. To eat, you put a child to stand guard. When the Italians came you hid the food, swallowed the mouthful. They were rude and greedy, and they didn't care about our island or the islanders; they used to cut down any tree for firewood. A tree can have a thousand years, five hundred years, such a tree is not to warm the backsides of pilfering swine.

'You see,' he announced, leaning back suddenly and laughing, 'Stavros didn't like the Italian garrison!'

He paused and took a gulp of his wine; then, as though remembering something truly distasteful, he spat the last of it across the floor.

'But when a man begs you for his life, then a man is a man, whoever and wherever he comes from. They came from the garrison where they were strong and treated us like dirt. They came one night crawling, bleeding, stunned. A man can die of arrogance, but he shouldn't die *for* it. So our Italian came, on the night of the massacre. He was freckled with blood and exhausted. The Germans would have killed him, but we took him in and sheltered him, and he lived here for two years. He was an officer, from Fiesole, in Tuscany, where the hills are blue.'

He paused now in his talk, and his reflective silence worked like a signal on the rest of the room, where three generations of women began to move like clockwork models with their keys released. The ancient, withered matron by the hearth was unceremoniously dragged into another corner, where she was left slumped like an old corn sack with only a few husks left in it. The others, three of them, all dressed in black, began to make their own preparations for a meal. Although the corn-sack granny was no longer by the fire, she continued to reach her wasted forearm out to one side of her and stir the air there as though stirring a pot. When her other hand rested from its exertions of fidgeting in the black folds of her dusty skirt, she would claw out with that as well, and poke at ashes that were not there, as though determined to go working to her grave, and so aware of how near she was to dying that she didn't feel safe unless she was continually doing something useful.

Behind me, the small shuttered window had filled with darkness, into which Stavros stared as though searching for the blueness of the Tuscan hills that he had heard so much about. He leaned towards me and demanded, 'You know what happened in Corfu?'

I shook my head, and he looked sad for me. I could see that if, without moving from his stone hut in the wood, he could talk to me of so many things and so well, it was disappointing that someone whose life was full of opportunity should turn up so ignorant on his doorstep. Notwithstanding, all I knew of Corfu was what Latin poets had written of it, and then Byron, and more lately, and more persistently, Thomas Cook. Stavros, looking up, seemed to read the words 'package tours' written across my eyes, because he sighed a little and then looked away, as if I had momentarily become an airport bus full of noisy fun-lovers on the way to ruin a beach. Looking down at our empty glasses brought back to him his own business of host, and filling both tumblers with wine he returned to the war and the fate of the Italian garrison on Corfu.

'Well,' he continued, 'you know that the Germans and the Italians were together. The Germans came here, and they didn't really have time to hold a whole island, even a small island like ours, so they left the soldiering to the Italians. Sometimes a German would come to visit. My brother saw a German general once in the town. But they came to check up, to tell off. Maybe that was why the Italians treated us so badly, because they got bullied too, and they passed it on. In my opinion, the power just went to their heads, like children with a big stick.

'To avoid corruption, the soldiers didn't stay very long, a few months maybe, then off to fight. Every time the garrison changed over, the Germans came to supervise the switch. That was when there were more soldiers on the island.

'The Germans separated the men from the officers one evening, and they took all the officers prisoner and locked them in the old fortress in Corfu town, in the dungeons. They took the men elsewhere. Next night, they led the officers out to the edge of the cliff, right there, in Corfu town, above, and they pushed them over into the sea. Two hundred officers. Italy had joined the English. They shared the garrison with the Germans, they were comrades, then Italy joins the English, but they never told the soldiers, they never told even the officers. So while Italy and England celebrate, their poor soldiers died. They didn't know what was happening. One minute they were eating my food in their fine rooms, then they were in prison, with no food or water for twenty-four hours, then they were being dashed against the rocks, drowning in the sea.

'The only ones to survive that night were the ones who were baptised with water.

'As for the common men, they had for them ships to take them away, prison ships. They took them out by night. It was a dark night, no moon. I remember the night because we heard the guns and we saw the planes circling over the island. As the soldiers waded out through the water, the planes began to fire on them, machine-gun fire. So the soldiers began to fall under the waves of bullets circling back and again, and they fell into the water, and they too were drowned.

'And do you know; it was the English trying to help us. They were English planes trying to stop the landing of a new garrison.

'As you can imagine, they panicked and ran and some were then killed by the Germans who waited on the beach and shot them. Others got away. But away — where can that be in the waters around an island? They had to swim or drift back in. They ran into the olive groves and hid. Sometimes people fed them there, and sometimes they hid them under their own house, like we did, or in out-of-the-way sheds.

'There was a bounty for every Italian handed in. Money is always tempting, and when you are hungry and your family is hungry it is more so. But if you see, day after day, the bodies of young men washed up on the beach, and hear so many stories of bodies all around the island washing in, and a young man asks you to save his life, and another orders you to sell it . . .'

He shrugged and licked his upper lip, pulling his moustache down and clipping it with his teeth.

'My Italian, he was a fine man. I found him in that shed

101

out there. My father took him in. It was his house. Alessandro lived in a pit in my room with my brothers and me. When the time was safe, he came out and we talked. He showed me how to speak his language, I showed him mine. He taught my brother to read and write. He helped. He always helped.

'After the war, he used to send things to us, for years and years. Once, just once, he came back to visit, but it made him cry. A lot of things used to make him cry. When he talked of his blue hills, he used to look out of that window behind your head and he would cry . . . and sometimes I could see the blue hills with him.

'I never want to leave this piece of land. I was lucky that he came to me here.'

I hardly had the time to take all this in, when Stavros jumped up again.

'Come,' he said, 'my brother will be waiting to take you to Corfu town. It is late. You must come again, next week, with your son. I will wait for you. I must sleep now, I am tired. I like to sleep.'

Then he slipped into Greek, and what I took to be his wife and mother joined him to say goodbye. There was no moon outside the door, just darkness, and the sound of birds resettling on their almond perches.

9

The marriage proposal of an angel

I caught the ferry back to Brindisi at nine o'clock in the morning, and although this now meant that I could successfully rendezvous at Sestri Levante station at the appropriate hour to collect my son, I was very sorry to be leaving the island of Corfu so soon after discovering it. Even the most hardened tourist would admit that fifty-eight hours of travelling deserved more than an overnight stay and a crack of dawn departure.

I had stayed the night in a small balconied hotel in a beautiful balconied street bearing all the grace and elegance of a once smart French town, with alleyways of strangely oriental shops on the one side, and public gardens, a fortress and the cliffs on the other. Stavros's brother, who had a smattering of Italian, invited me to rent his house for as long as I liked, and even offered to meet my returning ferry. I took up his offer of the house, unseen, for ten days, and I found his refusal to accept any payment in advance far more binding than a cheque.

The ferry turned out to be practically full. I wandered around the available decks a couple of times, wondering where to sit for the next twelve hours, and whom to sit next to, but could not reach any decision, so I stayed leaning over the rail of the ship watching the island recede in its wake. Years before, I had sailed to Venezuela thus, leaning over the rails of the upper deck watching the sea froth and churn below me, and watching the flying fish leap through the air with their phosphorescent wings catching the sunlight in the Caribbean. This was the Adriatic, and there were no flying fish, but the feel of the railings against my midriff felt the same, and the mood that came over me was similar.

The view of Corfu kept luring my eyes towards it. The Greeks and the Romans, the eighteenth-century lords and Thomas Cook and co. were all right. It was indeed a beautiful island. And, by chance, also staring out towards its shrinking shoreline was a beautiful young man. He had the kind of beauty usually associated only with statues or pictures. There was something ethereal about the stillness of his face. The clarity of his eyes, the perfect curves and arches of his brow and chin and his large dark golden curls gave him a truly angelic aspect.

As the ferry continued to cut through the sea, and Corfu became no more than a dot on the horizon, I continued to look out while leaning over the railings. Once in a while I stole a glance at this apparition, amazed that anyone of either sex could be so physically perfect. Each time I looked, I seemed to catch his eye, and each time I caught his eye, he blushed. He could have been in his early twenties or his early thirties, it was hard to tell which, but either way he was old enough to be embarrassed to be seen to be so embarrassed. Eventually, his silent blushes drove me back into the packed inner decks of the ship.

There was, by contrast, something very squalid about the profusion of legs and elbows inside. Only a few passengers had joined the ferry at Corfu, most of them with their container lorries. The rest of the passengers had come from Piraeus, Paxos and Antipaxos, and they had been living around the tables they sat at for two days. The tourists were, again, mostly Americans, and showed signs of having come from far afield. Each table had seats for four people, and each of these already had at least two, if not three or the full quota, people and at least as many bags beside or on top of it. The whole ship was full of legs – crumpled, uncomfortable, cramped legs stretching into every available space, and all doused heavily with eggshells and stale beer and sweat.

A long-legged girl knocked into me with three cans of fizzy orange in her hands. The orange froth spilled down me, and she was recalled by her tribe in voices that implied that 'Josephine' was prone to knock into people and things, and prone also to spilling drinks. I had passed the table that she was sitting at just seconds before, and she and her companions had seemed to be slumped under the most lethal apathy. However, her return with the spilt cans enlivened them to such a degree that they began to reminisce about other occasions across Eastern Europe when drinks had been dropped and their dropping remembered. Looking back at their table, the unsteady subject of their discussion smiled apologetically at me, seraphic in this litany of her talent. In the opposite direction, where there had been stacks of luggage and one man playing Patience, there was now a cleared seat and one man playing Patience. I sat down, and he greeted me in what I now, at least, recognised as Greek.

I took out my book and read, musing on why travel had become so sordid, and why there were so many people in the world, and why so many of them were on that particular ferry, and whether Josephine Baker had ever had to dig a place for her feet under a table full of cheese-parings and peeled eggshells, and why she had taken so many children on board on her travels, and whether mine would be all right, or would I too, like her, wind up on a doorstep outside a castle evicted for debt.

The man opposite me continued to play with his cards, but, as noon approached, more and more with one eye on the bar-room clock. Just before midday, he cleared the table and rummaged under the table for a long time, getting redder and redder in the face until he emerged triumphantly holding a starched white cloth which he spread over the vinyl top, and proceeded to lay for two. He made signs to me to see if I wanted to share his meal, and although I refused he continued to lay the table for two, pulling glasses and china, wine, fruit, salad, Wiener schnitzel and some pie-like things. Crowded as we were into the ship's bar, it looked incongruously elegant. One almost expected him to produce a fresh flower and make an arrangement for the centrepiece. I had just decided that I really should eat his picnic, now that he had taken so much trouble in laying it out, and was putting my book away accordingly, when Adonis from the upper deck came in, nodded to me, and squeezed in beside the other man, who turned out to be his uncle.

After much discussion between themselves, the uncle began the elaborate process of communication. It didn't take long to discover that the only language we had remotely in common was German, which he spoke with a heavy accent and I haltingly but fairly fluently as long as one didn't roam into the field of ideas. I was invited to lunch. Again I refused. They refused to eat if I didn't, so we ate together, and talked about this and that, and quickly became friends.

The uncle was a singer of Greek songs, and famous enough to have made several records, which he showed me; his nephew was a pianist. They were on their way to do a concert tour of Germany and their first concert would be in two days' time, in Frankfurt. They invited me to join them as their guest, to hear him sing. I told them I couldn't go. I had to collect my son, and now I had made plans to return to Greece. They liked the idea of my return, but were reluctant to abandon my accompanying them on their musical circuit. Sometimes they talked between themselves, the young man shy and earnest, the older very much at his ease and expansive. They seemed very fond of each other, and it was quite touching to see the deference that the nephew gave to his famous uncle and the affection that the uncle lavished on his childishly sweet nephew. After the meal we had brandies, and after the brandies we talked again.

The uncle, in particular, had a genius for separating the biographical details that I gave them into those that were genuine and those that I told them for convenience. It was as though he had a huge sieve that let the clear liquid through while keeping back the lumps. Between them they seemed to pinpoint my every weakness, and their precision made me feel uneasy. Sensing this, the uncle took out his cards, and, clearing the table, we played a Greek game that they taught me, for several hours. The game had dozens of nuances, signs and tricks that I couldn't fully grasp. After many dismal attempts to play at the same level as them, I gave up, leant back and slept.

I was awoken by the nephew, who had scarcely spoken to me, but who asked me now, in a very gentle voice, struggling with his scant knowledge of German, to stay awake because we had very little time to talk. He still wanted me to go with them to Germany. When it became clear to him that I would not, he sank his head into his hands and stayed like that for some minutes. Then he asked his uncle how many hours we had left to us, and when his uncle told him five, he groaned and retired into himself so far that he became almost invisible. Then it was his uncle's turn to plead once more for me to travel with them, and he unfolded their itinerary to me. As it turned out, they were travelling on the trans-Europe Notte, a night-train to Düsseldorf that I had to take as far as Bologna. I pointed this out to him and he relaxed a little, awakening his nephew from his trance-like state to tell him that we could add six and a half more hours on to our time.

Having woken me to ask me to stay awake and talk to him, the nephew now continued to slump with his head in his hands in a state of induced coma. I wondered if he might be ill, and so asked what was the matter with him. Since he could not or would not reply, I asked his uncle, who told me.

'It has come to him, and now he is ill. He has everything, because my sister married a fine wealthy man, and he is the only son. He has his mother who loves him, but his father is dead, drowned. So he has the property of his father even though he is a young man. It is all his, a big house by the sea, so that you walk from the windows across the verandah to the water, and olive trees and grapes. And he can play the piano, always he could play the piano, as though it were not him, but something going through him. Other times, I take another pianist with me to tour, once only my nephew came. That was the best tour. He was only a boy then, but he plays best for me, and we are friends. This time he came because I am tired, and getting a little older now, so it tires me to tour. He will look after me, he is good and kind. Only now he wants to turn back if you do not come. He wants you to come. It has come to him and it can never go away. All the villages around where he lives know him. Look at him, he is beautiful. All the girls see him, tall and still, and they love him. He takes them out for an evening, a day, and then . . . finish.'

Here the uncle dusted his hands as though dispatching the hordes of eager maidens from him.

'Never, never, do the girls go back to his house. Never. Now it has come to him. He wants to marry you, he wants you to go back to his island, take his house, all that he has, my nephew loves you. He asks you to marry him. He is afraid you will go. He is sick in his heart.'

I couldn't think of a single thing to say to this second-hand proposal. On the one hand it was utterly ridiculous; on the other it was so bizarre that I found it alarmingly attractive. In a great gesture of cowardice I excused myself and went to the loo, where I stayed for the best part of half an hour. Things have to be pretty serious to stay in a ship's bathroom for that long, but I was feeling upstaged. I was Miss Impulsive, or, rather, Mrs Impulsive, since I had now, nominally, been married for fifteen years in all. Suddenly I was becoming the voice of caution, the hanger-back. I went out and up on deck and took up my position over the railings, looking into the sea to find out what the troubled spume had to say about all these goings on. They seemed to beat out a message which was loud and clear in whatever language one spoke. I had married my first husband because he was beautiful and mysterious and had asked me to out of the blue and then insisted. He also suffered so deeply when I turned him down that I ultimately accepted, if only to save him from such pain and grief. It had taken me nine years to extricate myself from that marriage, and who knew how many more to recover from the loneliness of being married to and living with a complete stranger.

The nephew came up behind me, touched my shoulder, and then stood beside me, leaning over the railings too. I don't know what the waves were telling him, or, indeed, if he was listening to them, but they kept on pounding out the same message to me, defining it now as five simple words beating in against the ship's side: *Leave the train at Bologna.*

We arrived in Brindisi just as we had left Corfu, with the two of us watching the sea, while I simultaneously watched the mainland and stole odd glances at him, which made him blush; and he stared strangely at me, feeling, I felt, either sick in his heart or sick in his head.

*   *   *

At the beginning of its journey along the Adriatic coast, the night train through Europe's only concession to the idea of long-distance travel is the names that it slots on to the sides of its carriages. Inside, the train is just the usual string of compartments, a few of which convert into untended bunks, but many of which don't. Outside, it is like a great articulated gecko in a dusty blue skin, disjointing itself through the night and discarding the bits. So one carriage will be shunted away to Copenhagen, another to Amsterdam, another to Spain, to Turkey, to France, to Switzerland, and the small remaining vital core will eventually find its way to Düsseldorf, hence its subtitle of the Düsseldorf Express.

Its passengers at Brindisi are mostly from the incoming ferries. Out of season, these dock only on alternate days, so there are, accordingly, alternate days when the Düsseldorf Express starts its journey relatively empty. In the holiday season, when the ferries sail in daily to the port of Brindisi and unload what look like impossibly large loads of passengers who emerge from its bowels like a steaming human froth, the Düsseldorf Express is correspondingly and nightmarishly full.

Its passengers range from the disbelieving to the discontented to the incensed. More than any other train in Europe, it seems to give one a sense of being cheated. People try to charge it under the trade descriptions act. Travelling nowadays across the Channel, people seem to have become resigned to the fact that there is scarcely ever a restaurant car across France on the trains from Boulogne and Calais. If there is, one is pleasantly surprised. If there isn't, the small hamper comes into its own. Then again, I have seen people disappointed by the absence of any drinking water on these trains, and, at times, even gasping in the night for something to drink. But the name fits the train. Thus the boat train doesn't drop people in the middle of Leeds, or on the inland parts of the Kent countryside, it takes them to a boat, or at worst, the dock where they can catch one. And the Naples Express, the 210 of which I am so fond, is fast, if little else, and does come and go to Naples. The train that goes from Calais to Milan Central pretends to do nothing else: it is not advertised as the Gourmet Special, or the Bistro Bonanza, so one arrives in Milan without the sense of having been taken, so to speak, for a ride. Right from the start, before there has even been so much as a shunting from the station, the Düsseldorf Express looks as though it were wearing a disguise.

A couple of hundred tourists have been funnelled off the ferry and have marched, as though in a demonstration, up the main street of Brindisi, with backpacks for placards. They show every sign of having survived arduous and intrepid experiences. Enamel mugs and coffee-pots hang ostentatiously from the straps of their voluminous luggage. They give the impression sometimes of having spent much of their travels trying to stamp some outward mark of the places they have been to on their persons. So they also wear Tibetan caps, tonsured hair, fakir-length fingernails and a number of other cosmetic tricks ranging from views of the Taj Mahal tattooed on their cheeks to discarded python skins wrapped around their necks. All this is meant to give the clear impression that they have just returned like so many Marco Polos from the East. Their luggage has often become huge ethnic baskets instead of backpacks. They have ways of making you believe that they have come from India (whether in fact they have or not). The image is all-important. Perhaps that is why the disappointment is so immense when the train that is to bear them back to their despised ones is so uncivilised.

Just as it is the Americans, with their long legs and their transatlantic confidence, who stride ahead through the town, so it is the Americans who tend to take the lead in their disapproval of the train. When they are in the desert (man), they can just lie out on sand under the stars; but when a train calls itself an international express, it should at least look like one.

Passengers are coaxed in by the guards, who try hard to persuade them that all is well and that, despite its provincial appearances, this train really will take them to Copenhagen, or Amsterdam, or Geneva. Some people, particularly the older ones, just refuse to board it, believing that there must be a better one if only they wait. So they do just that, only to find that Brindisi is a long way from anywhere, especially by night, and, unwillingly, that their only alternative is to wait until the next evening and catch the same thing and follow the same route, but with the extra bitterness of having their European programme thrown out by twenty-four hours.

The real trouble begins after the train leaves the station. While it is still at the platform, the guards can say that it really is an express. Once it begins to crawl through the night, practically bump-starting at every out-of-the-way station along the Adriatic coast and then creeping inland, like a sick centipede, on its way to Bologna, there is no avoiding the deceit. It is night, and the places have strange names and desolate platforms. The corridors vibrate to the complaints of travellers hijacked by the night. People are tortured by the pace. Many a clogged artery clogs a little more as the Düsseldorf Express creeps through the Italian night, moving sometimes no faster than a decrepit old man, crippled and limping on ill-fitting artificial limbs.

Gradually, as bits of the original train are disconnected at the most unlikely stations, and proper carriages from other trains are linked up to the skeleton, the snail to Düsseldorf takes on at least the semblance of a proper express, even though it continues to feel its way through the night. At Bologna, it waits for an hour, during which time it breaks out of its maggoty chrysalis, emerging into the darkness of Reggio Emilia a fully winged creature to speed its way on through the Alps. I was to leave the train at Bologna. I had to leave the train at Bologna. All the way there, I reminded myself of this, because all the way there, much more than on the boat, I felt myself being swept off my feet.

As the nephew and I had followed the procession of passengers up the main street of Brindisi, his uncle had darted on ahead to procure seats. The sense of being borne by the crowd was so overpowering that it made me feel silly, as did my walking beside this man who insisted on considering himself engaged to be married, and who was a little out of sorts because of the failure, on my part, to sort out the terms of the agreement. Then a bar seemed to beckon to me as we passed its open door, and I dived in, quickly followed by the staggeringly beautiful, but very confused, nephew.

It flashed through my mind, for the first time, that although we were such excellent friends now, the Greek musicians and I, and although I fully intended to disembark at Bologna, there was the chance that they might not let me. I didn't know. It all seemed a bit far-fetched, and I doused the thought with a double brandy. Through the bottom of my glass I spied a familiar face entering the bar, quickly followed by another. These were two of the three men I had met, lunched with, drunk with, and been shown the not inconsiderable sights of the city of Brindisi by, on my way through to Greece, just three days before. I had forgotten their kindness in escorting me to the ferry, and also their equally kind offer of meeting the ferries back the following week to have a drink and take me to my train with a proper and fitting farewell. I was just rummaging around in my brain for a suitable apology and trying to organise an introduction, furnish an explanation and invite them to join us, when the epitome of human beauty solved the problem for me by intimating through some very expressive facial movements that both of the two newcomers could scram. They looked at me, counting on me, I saw, to introduce them for what they were: friendly dolphins and not sharks. I stood up to do so, reaching out my hand to shake theirs. The nephew also rose to his feet and, stepping between me and the newcomers with the agility of a dancer but the ferocity of a wolverine, caused them to leave me mid-sentence, while the proprietorial pianist muttered something about there being no time.

The Greek uncle had found a compartment of his own, and having laid out a dinner for three on his damask napiery he was leaning through the window, looking out for the happy couple-to-be. The train left late, as it often does, due to the grumbling and harassment of its human cargo, and shuddered out of old Brindisium with a series of spasmodic jerks.

Christ may have stopped at Eboli, but the guidebooks all stopped before Brindisi, leaving it with its ferries and its

Roman remains stranded inside its palings of peach and almond blossoms, and peaches and almonds themselves, with its secrets kept and its spirits unspoiled. Shunting through the spectral empty stations of the Adriatic coast in the middle of the night and the small hours of the morning grants the passing tourist no impression of the wild beauty of the dunes and the savage hills behind them. Bari and Foggia, Termoli and Vasto are just names in the night, and a sleepless one at that. Even places like Pescara, where the poet d'Annunzio was born, or Ancona, with its high cathedral built on the site of the temple of Venus, pass unnoticed. Rossini's Pesaro holds no arias; and Rimini, the littered cluttered villain of that coast, slides by under the same anonymous blanket as everywhere else on the line.

All through the heavily veiled Molise and the equally impenetrable Abruzzi, my marriage to the nephew and my Greek future were discussed in pidgin German. Neither of them would accept my adamant refusal. 'We are in the hands of destiny,' they told me, and I had no choice. I remembered the windy bus-stop on the edge of Clapham Common where my first husband had proposed to me, and I remembered that he too had called it *la fuerza del destino*. One had to be careful of destiny; she has a lot to answer for.

'You don't need to love him,' the uncle insisted in his strange German dialect. 'He loves you.'

The discussion was endless, and endlessly repetitive. I dragged in Iseult and Alexander as blocking pawns, but the nephew loved children. He had never seen them, I said. He didn't need to, I was told, he had seen me, and that was enough. I dragged in the madness of my family, and its total unsuitability as a credential for marriage. I threw enough sand on the scheme to have flattened the dunes from Brindisi to Otranto. The nephew, who had never wanted to marry before, wanted to marry me, now. I told him a hundred times, if I told him once, that I was already married. They would pay for my divorce, they would pay for my upkeep and that of my children and the seven imaginary sisters that I had invented in place of my three actual ones. Money was no problem. I was being brainwashed into believing nothing was a problem. The more tender and emotional they became, the more I felt that I might have a real problem trying to get off the train: an emotional holocaust was brewing, and I was to blame.

Had I not absolutely had to meet young Alexander by a given hour that day, I would have jumped the train at Pescara when it stopped there and cut short the flaying of the nephew's nerves. However, I had promised to arrive, and left it too late to make a later rendezvous, so I had no choice but to catch my connection at Bologna. The train stopped for a long time at Pescara, over an hour, and the distraught uncle went in and out to the corridor to smoke. In between their joint entreaties to me, mostly voiced through the senior partner, they had fierce whispered arguments in Greek. It seemed that the nephew was refusing to go to Germany if I insisted on leaving the train at Bologna. I could see it was a good ploy; it had worked for lunch, why not now?

The uncle was in the corridor under a great halo of Karelia smoke. His beatific nephew was sitting opposite me invoking the god of destiny by repeating, 'Kommst du mit mir' in what sounded like a slowed down Gregorian chant.

Then, quite unexpectedly, he said, in English, 'Are you with me?'

Not a word of English had been spoken all day or night. Perhaps that was all he knew, conjured up from some advertisement or remembered phrase. The train pulled out of Pescara at that moment, reminding me of its satyric, illustrious and eccentric son, Gabriele d'Annunzio. Marching to take Fiume after the First World War, with a band of rebel soldiers all ready to die, he had said, 'Those who are not with me are against me.'

As we crawled back into the night, leaving the dimly lit station behind us, the words seemed to take on a curious, almost sinister connotation. The train lurched, and the sliding door to our compartment slid shut. Looking up, I caught a glimpse of the nephew's eyes; they were hurt and flickering with something that looked like anger. I felt afraid, with an indefinable fear. I began to watch him closely now, avoiding his eyes. He pulled out a bag from under his seat with the heels of his feet, and then, still watching me, he plunged his hand inside it, bringing out a broad twelve-inch knife. I watched it with dread. It was double-edged. He held it for a moment, saying nothing, but with his knuckles clenched so tightly round the blade that they went white. In my mind, I had already died.

Five years before, in Paris, someone had tried to strangle me. I fainted then and escaped with only a necklace of bruises round my neck and a phobia about even the gentlest touch on my throat. At the time of the strangling, I realised, some seconds before it happened, that that was what was in the air. I had felt the same chill numb terror as I felt now. I was overwhelmed by my own idiocy, and I felt a pain in my lungs at the thought of my two children, followed by a smell of mimosa which was to blossom in six weeks' time.

Then he took out an apple and began to slice it, and offered me a sliver, which I took, trying not to let him see how much my hands were shaking. I moved across to the far corner of the compartment, near the door, and pretended to sleep.

He continued to play with his knife, stroking the blade and staring with an expression of crazed innocence on his face. I stole glances at him, but felt intuitively that if I said the wrong thing, he'd stab me. After what seemed like many minutes, he picked up his apple again, and continued to eat it. The moment seemed to have passed, whatever it was, and I, drained by my recent fear and the adrenalin that had pumped round my body in the last three minutes reasoned that if he was going to kill me, I'd rather he did it in my sleep; and if he wasn't, I was tired anyway.

I woke to see a dimly lit sign announcing our arrival at a place called Civitanova. The nephew was sitting beside me, his uncle stretched out across three seats in front. His grasp of German seemed a lot better than it had been all day, as though he had either been practising while I slept, or his mind had simply cleared in the interval. He asked me not to sleep, but to take pity on his pain, and he asked me not to agree to a marriage but at least to promise to go to Germany within the week to see him. I agreed to both these things, and he was so pleased he wept. Although he didn't know it, I would have agreed to practically anything by then.

I come from a totally paranoid family. My grandmother was so paranoid that she believed in a world conspiracy to undo her, like a piece of knitting that life was unravelling on a daily basis. My mother was paranoid, my sisters are paranoid, my daughter is paranoid – even my two-year-old son was paranoid. We all think we are being watched. In our calmer moments we realise and accept that we actually are being watched, or rather noticed, and this contributes and possibly creates that constant sense of surveillance. I cannot bear to walk in the dark with anyone behind me, just as I cannot bear to drive, day or night, with another car behind me. Most of the time, I can talk myself out of my uneasiness and let it pass. But having been half strangled once, kidnapped once, and attacked a couple of times, when I feel a real sense of threat I follow my tardy instincts and become as spinelessly accommodating as the situation demands. Had the uncle been a priest or judge, I would have become a bigamist then and there if I felt that it increased my chances of leaving the compartment in one piece.

For the two hundred kilometres from Ancona to Bologna the nephew sat beside me, showing no signs of violence, no restless fingers, no wires or blades. He asked me to hold his hand, which I did, and was strangely comforted by his touch. After Rimini he cried silently, some of his tears finding their way on to the inside of my wrist. At Casena he awakened his uncle and whispered to him in Greek, whereupon his uncle rummaged in his coat and produced a notebook, address book and a pen. He wrote out some half a dozen addresses and telephone numbers in Frankfurt, explaining who each person was and how to arrive at the place or leave a message. They had already given me their Greek addresses, but he gave them to me again, adding those of cousins and neighbours to enable me to arrive there if need be. Then he slept again, I think more out of genuine exhaustion than any desire to leave us on our own. The nephew's head had long been leaning on my shoulder. As the train rocked into Bologna, I realised that he was sleeping too.

I got up, took my miniature suitcase and opened the door practically in one movement. They awoke, the nephew tumbling into the space where my shoulder had been. The bright lights and the noise on the platform outside spoke for themselves. They said nothing, and neither did I. I held my hand up as a token farewell, and left. Once on the platform I hurried towards the steps that would lead me away. I was aware, without looking, that they had come to the window. I felt their presence over my head as I walked by. Before I reached the steps I heard my name called, and then again. The second call reminded me of the strangled cry of a woman in Venezuela at the moment when her dead son was carried out in his coffin. I walked on. It came again, alarming all the other passengers, who turned to look. Then I turned back, guided by a surge of memory and emotion to where they hung leaning from the window.

The uncle was crying for his nephew, the nephew was weeping for himself, and I was crying too, I don't know why or for whom. I gave my suitor back the hand that I had stolen from him in the train, and he held it until all the blood drained out of my arm raised to meet his.

The whistles blew, and the uncle made me promise again to come to Frankfurt, which I did, knowing that I wouldn't go.

'If you don't come, in two weeks we come to find you,' he said, and I smiled, feeling lousy, but safe in having given them the wrong address in Liguria. As the whistles blew, I saw only their kindness and concern and the really astonishing beauty of my new fiancé.

The whistles blew again, and the guard with the red luminous lollipop waved the train out of the station. The gathering motion wrenched our fingers apart, scattering tears over mine. I had two hours to wait until my next train. It took me a while to stop crying, and then I slept, fitfully, in the bleak waiting room, thinking, each time I woke, that they had both been right in a way, when they called it destiny, for it was my destiny to be loved by strangers.

10

Tangoing between partners:
Nice to Altnabreac

It was February 1985, fifteen years since Bologna had been the centre of my world. I had lived there, in an attic flat in a fourteenth-century building with a landing like a garden where the neighbours gathered to dissect and label their world, and with an inner courtyard, below, that was always full of wool to be carded.

I had not been back – have never been back – never, that is, further than the railway station. I suppose I feel that it might all have changed, and I treasure my memory of it so fondly that I don't want to bear the disappointment of missing anything: of finding the city lacking, falling below the dream-city in my mind. The two old ladies who lived opposite me, and who tempered my loneliness with their obsolete royal gossip, are probably dead by now, and yet by not returning I can still believe and hope that they are not.

When I lived there, the station was a crucial part of my life. I was always coming or going or meeting someone there. And once, for several days, when a chain of mishaps befell me and I was rendered homeless and had to remain hidden, I lived there, sleeping in the Ladies and the waiting room. It was all as familiar to me as a childhood haunt. In 1980 a terrorist bomb destroyed the station, killing over eighty people in one of the worst atrocities of its kind in Europe. Now it has been rebuilt, all changed, and all charged with sad memories, for the people who work there and for the city itself, of that gratuitous violence. In 1984 an express train crashed just outside it, and again dozens of people died. Something like eighty-four bodies were picked out of the debris.

I want to go back to Bologna, if I go at all, to pick over my

118

own personal memories, but it seems tasteless, in the light of such public grief, to be concerned (on the same site) with my own infinitesimal losses. Then again, seeing the station building so altered increased my dread of finding, in place of the great Renaissance capital with its graceful palaces and its beautiful churches, a concrete monstrosity of apartment blocks and offices. So although I have been through Bologna literally dozens of times, I have never left the station, never even looked outside, and, maybe, never shall.

After sleeping off my Greek proposal in the waiting room, I left Bologna Central, picked up my son in Sestri Levante, and then went with him back to Greece, but only as far as Corfu. We were there within a week of my having left it, and after ten days of lying in its wintry sun on empty beaches, and traipsing, under happier circumstances, through its ancient olive groves, I returned to Italy.

Now I found myself in a phase of manic restlessness in which I used the railways like an emergency extension to my own nervous system. For this, I chose the line from Bologna to Brindisi, travelling backwards and forwards, occasionally taking a day or so off in Brindisi, for the best part of three weeks. The two-year-old Alexander travelled with me, with his monosyllabic vocabulary, his teddy bear, his luggage, and his own, younger, passion for trains.

Looking back, that time that I spent literally on the rails may appear to be the nearest I ever came to going off them. But at the time we gave every appearance of calm, enjoying the views, the pear juice and the sandwiches more than on many other occasions. We always had a sleeping compartment, and it was often to ourselves. I read a lot, Alexander perfected his bilingual pronunciation of a number of short words, and although he was not any good at his own conversation, he showed every sign of enjoying mine (although this may merely have been expedient politeness).

To travel anywhere with a small child in Italy is like having a passport to everyone's heart. When the child has long golden curls, and is a boy, and fits the rather bizarre notion of what the young Christ looked like, there is never any lack of disinterested companionship.

119

OFF THE RAILS

I could have gone back to Greece, back to Corfu; the house was offered there, the people were kind and it had even stopped raining for the ten days of our stay. But always when I arrived in Brindisi and set off down the one road to the docks, the time seemed wrong. I still had Italianitis, that strange, chronic, often acute, and sometimes fatal disease that ties the victim to a love of Italy.

Somewhere in Sestri Levante my trunks were waiting, packed, half of them to be taken into the hills to a village called Velva where I had rented a house, and half to be rail-freighted to London. I was due back in England in early April, but I still wasn't ready to go, so I yo-yoed up and down the Adriatic Line, clinging to Italy in my metal cocoon, absolved of any resonsibility beyond the confines of the corridor, safe as a hermit crab inside its shell.

Twice I doubled back to Sestri Levante to see Enrico and drink coffee in the Bar Jolly opposite the station, and to see Alexander's nanny and show that my charge was quite well, and even flourishing. Whenever I take to excessive travelling I camouflage it under the general term of business, and thus disguise some of its more eccentric aspects. Thus, much of my brief stop-overs were taken up by enquiries into how this imaginary business was going and when it would come to an end. Once, during those three weeks, we went to Milan, but that was merely because I fell asleep and missed our usual station.

Gradually, where once I had pretended to be away on business when I travelled, I began to take my typewriter with me and really did get down to some, stopping in small hotels for a week here and a week there, writing as I went along. I travelled across the black rail-lines of maps across France, Switzerland, Italy, Holland and Spain. I felt aimless but sane. I became a connoisseur of old hotels.

Gone were the days when Karl Baedeker guided his readers to the Royal Victoria Hotel in Pisa where rooms were 3s 2½d. That was in 1909, when the Royal Victoria was the finest hotel in Tuscany. Now it is slightly run down, and therefore in many ways completely unspoiled, and although it costs more than the three shillings of the guide, it is still one of the most absurdly cheap places to stay at and still has some of the loveliest rooms. The Duke of Wellington's suite, for instance, is exactly as it was when the old duke stayed there, with its hand-painted furniture, crests and drapes. Upstairs there is some magnificent furniture. The Arno glides its green waters by in front of the windows, the leaning tower tilts behind, the horse-drawn carriages clatter beside it, and over the bridge, the Ponte di Mezzo, out of sight but not out of walking distance, is the station with its access to the metal artery, pumping, pumping, to Florence and Rome and Naples, to Paris and Venice and Nice.

A headscarf and shades and a Grace Kelly car – these are the main requisites for a trip to the French Riviera, and long legs and a smattering of French. Armed with all this, and an extra trunk of miscellaneous extras for luck, I arrived in Nice very much in the spirit in which it was built. Enter a latterday flapper with a social conscience and a shallow interest in archaeological remains.

From the high road, by night, Nice lies like a massive field of fireflies hovering over summer corn. By day, the size of the city is disguised by the brilliance of its shore. Only by night, and the quantity of lights, is there any clue to the extent of its seething hinterland, and even then, on approaching the coast, the wide boulevards outshine the flickering glow of the hundreds of streets that lead back into the hills. The seafront is as radiant by night as the illuminated wing of a flying fish poised in its flight from the glittering sea.

In nearby Grasse – world centre of the perfume industry, thanks to a fashion begun by the Medici family in the sixteenth century of scenting their gloves – thousands of tons of flowers are distilled every year. Perhaps the doormen's gloves are scented too. Much later, in 1798, Napoleon began his Italian campaign from Nice. Since he was known to have a penchant for dousing his horse with aromatic oils, perhaps he chose Nice, in part, for its nearness to the scented city.

Nice has been invaded and reinvaded through the centuries. In the last two centuries it is the invasion of the English aristocracy, and the Russian royal family, and the untitled monarchs of the arts, that has left the greatest impression on this perennially generous host. Nice and Cannes were rival watering towns, each with their warm winter season, but it was Nice that became the richest jewel in the Riviera's tiara, aided by the arrival and endorsement of Queen Victoria herself. The Hotel Regina was named in her honour, and the other great hotels were built in her wake.

Not far away was the base of the Imperial Russian Navy, and Tsar Nicholas II travelled down regularly from St Petersburg in a private railway car to patronise the new hotels and, later, to reside in his own villa at Cimiez. The Russians brought with them their characteristic daring and excess. Each week the Tsar's gardens were renewed, with teams of gardeners working through the night to plant his flowerbeds with different displays. To the scandal of the prim English, and still managing to shock the less prim French, the Grand Duchess herself insisted on taking her daily bath naked in her stableyard, with her cavalry horses (facing discreetly outwards) standing in a square to shield her from the many prying eyes.

The Romanov millions spilled into buildings and paintings, and, from 1903, on the Boulevard Tsarevich, into a Russian Orthodox Cathedral. But it was the English who pre-dominated, on their own fashionable promenade.

Henri Négresco dreamed of a hotel that would be like a palace, fit for princes. The sun, after centuries of being shunned, was finally reprieved, and so the Hotel Négresco, flagship of Nice's great hotels, faced south and out to sea, occupying an entire block of the already famous Promenade des Anglais. He died of cancer and ruin, but his name still strikes chords of splendour and luxury. The name of the Reverend Lewis Way does not stir the imagination or quicken the blood, but it was he who cleared, single-handed, a path six foot wide and four and a half miles long, through thick bracken, along the coast. It was christened 'The Englishman's Way' at the time, and later became one of the most fashionable promenades in Europe. Now it is the spine of the English skeleton that can be unearthed in Nice.

It was here that Isadora Duncan regained her waning

122

fame. Swathed in her habitual silks and trailing scarves, she was driven down the promenade in a magnificent Bugatti. But her long scarf was chewed by a back wheel, and she was strangled. For once, not even her critics could accuse her of having devised a mere publicity stunt. Her autobiography, published posthumously, contains many entries beginning 'Hotel Négresco . . .'.

Isadora Duncan used to practise her dances in the cupola room. I practise my tango steps on my white marble balcony under the gaze of a disapproving seagull. I feel an unaccustomed urge to grow old, and degenerate into a heap of treasured silks, and end my days in the surreal splendour of this gilded catacomb. Viva the long scarves, and the Bugatti. I have come in a poor replica of a 1926 Bugatti, but could find nowhere to park it. Once slotted, it is abandoned, and the stainless-steel shimmer of the train is adopted, with its webbed network of track.

The key to Nice is in its heart. The heart of Nice has been preserved on a life-support system, tended by dozens of skilled hands, at the Négresco. It is another evening, and after a successful skirmish through the wines I make my choice from the menu and my appetite flatters the chef. Between courses, I study the geology of the dining room, which once was socially stratified, with royalty in the front line, by the windows with the sea view. In the second row, peers of lesser titles and their spouses would be seated. After these dukes and counts came the captains of industry, merchants and celebrities, and in the fourth row the lesser mortals. Each row of guests was served by its own waiters. A waiter would begin on the lowly row four, and after a year he would be allowed to serve the industrialists. After another year he would be promoted to the noblemen, and only after four years would he be eligible to pour a prince's gravy. Year five would see a waiter as a captain, monitoring the other staff on the back table. So a man would work his way through the strata until, after sixteen years, he graduated to *maître d'hôtel*.

The dining room is now much changed, keeping pace with a society that no longer acknowledges an order of precedence

– not even the ancient precedence of respect for the old prevailing within the four walls of the world of the 1980s. The social carousel is mirrored now only in the décor of the annexed Rotonde. With its legacy of excellence, though, the Négresco bears signs neither of fossilisation nor of the ravages suffered by the other great hotels that have been forced to decline or succumb to the guest-factory syndrome.

This structured fantasy, which once was host to Chagall and Matisse, Scott Fitzgerald, Maugham and Hemingway, Alfred Hitchcock and James Dean, and a bestiary of brilliance from the spheres of the arts, be they pianist of the calibre of Rubenstein or singers of the poignancy of Piaf, still wraps the world's great artistes in its luxurious folds. The distinguished Augiers are its sponsors, with Madame Augier as the patron saint of its survival and Michel Palmer the impresario of its success.

The English and Russian revellers have long since gone from Nice, but the party continues without them. It is still a place of great operas and exhibitions, of theatres and concerts and cabarets. Although in London the fashionable intelligence no longer dictates a warm winter season in Nice to its courtiers, the city continues to flourish without it. In the high season of the summer, the elegance of old Nice is in partial eclipse, over-shadowed by the sameness of beach tourists anywhere. If only Verdi had given *La Traviata* a happy ending, Nice would be like its wayward heroine. Perhaps, in terms of the English occupancy of this great city, it still is. For the arias born of that great love affair hang in the air, and the sumptuous surroundings remain, as do the balls and the banquets; the gypsies are played by the Carnival, with its frenzy of costumes and colours and flowers; and Violetta, the beautiful, ailing heroine, dies in song and cannot be forgotten. In November, Nice is full of violets. Vendors sell them in shops and stalls, together with sprays of feathery mimosa. But more than any other flower, here, in a maze of streets each balconied and festooned, and in the flower market itself, with its lingering bouquet of heavy scents, the cornflower dominates in November, standing, as does the poppy in England, for the fields of

France, for the Great War, on the ground where so much of it was fought.

Millions of years ago, the whole of the Côte D'Azur lay under the sea. Now it merely lies under its influence, ruled by its damascene blues and greens highlighted by turquoise and lapis lazuli. It is a silent ruler, whispering as its broderie hemline is drawn across the shingle beach. There follows, geologically, the Promenade des Anglais with its rich vein of great hotels, the Masséna Museum, the disused casino. Next come the musical streets, rue Verdi and rue Rossini and a great many others, drawing one back into the old town and Cimiez, the old residential centre, with its Roman remains and more recent Russian reliquary. On and on the layers continue, through the balconied hive of a huge city. Notwithstanding, the seafront and its immediate hinterland continue to be the stage upon which the city's image lives. It is like its own opera house, painted and decorated and gilded and rouged, with great theatre curtains screening the stagehands and props from the audience.

The days of the private Russian trains have passed with the days of the English milords. These days a miniature train takes tourists and geriatrics and geriatric tourists around town for joy rides in the sun. The real trains now are silver container trains, articulated aluminium crates that glint even in the winter light. From a distance, they look like space-age cattle trucks, shuttling backwards and forwards along the coast – Cannes, Antibes, Fréjus, Nice. For me, the Riviera means Italy and Levanto, Sestri Levante, Genoa, but I know that for most people it is here in Provence. I felt a need to dent the surface of the pool to see the water; to find more signs of the last colonists.

Every time I looked out across the Baie des Anges, leaning over the white marble balcony of my bedroom, it intrigued me to see the Promenade des Anglais with its high palms, and the narrow shoreline with its flattened pebbles, all unchanged, and with only the English visitors so categorically withdrawn. Where had they gone? I know, from long experience, that it is useless to ask academic questions of the sea. So I repaired instead to the English graveyard, a sad and

shady place cramped to one side of the small grey English
Church. It was pathetically small, which is a tribute to the
salutary climate of Nice. It was filled almost entirely by
reverends and officers whose tombs are subsiding into the
soil like so many launchings of ships to death. Untended, and
overgrown, with yews and cypresses, it is dark and dank
there. The ground has a fen-like sogginess. Although there
are only a few graves, some of them still contrive to be
inaccessible, obliging one to walk across the inscriptions on
the tombs. Because of the subsidence, most of the stonework
is cracked or broken, and these vestiges of the British
presence seem to be disappearing beneath the weight of a
more recent settlement that has all but forgotten them. They
have sunk into the soil with an almost indecent haste.
Already many of the names and most of the epitaphs are
buried with their mortal remains. Soon the archaeologists
who have laboured at Cimiez with the traces of Greek and
Roman and Ligurian habitation will be the only ones able to
unearth these, the only tourist captains to go down with their
ship.

The roll-call of Nice reads like an alphabet of fame. The
English graveyard had one small noticeboard at the head of
its second and last short alley announcing the resting place of
their most famous guest, the vicar who wrote the hymn
'Abide With Me'. Without this noticeboard, visitors could
speculate on the varying degrees of fame of the unknown
dwellers of the sunken tombs; with it, it is clear that
whatever greatness of spirit, given directly or vicariously to
this Riviera town by the migratory English flocks who came
here once a year for nearly a century, was left in the town,
and not hidden in this damp cemetery. Ironically, the turf
that 'Abide With Me' is remembered for is not that under
which its writer lies, but the far-away, less (or more) sacred
turf of Wembley, where his words are sung each year at Cup
Finals. Perhaps the key to the English decline lies in another
graveyard: the War Cemetery, where a generation of
potential fun-lovers must lie.

The great hotels of the Promenade des Anglais still serve
champagne by the bucketful, but the slippers are now worn

by aged Russian ladies who shuffle their way to the
Orthodox Cathedral in Cimiez, and pay their last obeisance
to a dying religion, in a place where their dreams have
already died.

The incense burns and smothers an interior redolent of
William Burges, crammed full of candles and icons. The
seven old women and the two old men make their Sunday
pilgrimage past the rows of icons, alternately bowing from
the waist to touch the ground and kissing the painted saints.
Given their age and their advanced decrepitude, it seems a
remarkable act of faith to have such suppleness. They bear
witness to the times that Monsieur Augier will write about in
his book *When the Grand Dukes Danced at Nice*. Some of
them may even have danced as the grand dukes' partners.
But all that is left now is their imperious habit of whispering
through concerts. They whisper now, relentlessly, through
the service. The ritual singing and chanting carries the
morning through its ritual stages. A young acolyte carrying
an enormous candle round the golden honeycomb of an altar
fails to withdraw at the appropriate time and is finally
chivvied away by his elderly counterpart. The bronchitic
priest coughs his way through his otherwise beautifully sung
lines, and the congregation warble their response.

Despite the whispered gossip and the slow, rheumatic
shuffling of the faithful, who seemed more intent on lighting
their many yellow candles than on paying attention to their
priest, this service seemed so intimate that I withdrew before
the end. One tiny, shrivelled lady had hovered at the back
with me, among the pastel-painted flowers of the entrance.
All through the service she sang with a sweet, lark-like voice,
following the responses with an entranced expression on her
face. On leaving, I was gathered back into the world by the
sunlight, but the frail, beautiful voice of the ancient crone
followed me down the steps and past the incredibly ornate
onion domes of the cathedral.

Outside, the streets had the emptiness of a Sunday
morning suburb. The painted roses of the Tsar's villa had
long since been uprooted and covered in concrete. The villa
itself is now a clinic. The Russians and the English have, to

all intents and purposes, gone, but the great skeleton of their having been there remains, and the sun remains, and the people of Nice now dance without them.

> Move him into the sun –
> Gently its touch awoke him once . . .
> Always it woke him, even in France . . .

Meanwhile, on my intermittent returns to England, life continued apace. I was never quite sure at what pace, and had even taken tango lessons to see if I couldn't somehow slot into the right stance at the right time. From the spring of 1985 to the spring of 1987 I commuted between England and the Riviera, spending two British weeks to each four Italian.

One by one the different cities opened like buds warming to the first days of spring. I began not just to travel up and down the lines, but to get off at stations other than the ones marked as my destination on the ticket. Florence and Lucca and Siena all became more than mere names to conjure with. I was appalled at how little I knew of Italy, even the bits that I lived in. It had become a landscape of names. Even Liguria, and Genoa itself, I knew only as a personalised catechism. So there was Genova Sesto, Genova Principe, Genova Brignole, Genova Nervi, Genova Quarto. Everywhere had come to be a station sign, and places made sense in the broader map of the entire line. And the names themselves, I think, had lost their meaning, and, at times, their sound. I began to reawaken to the world. I was no longer sleepwalking, I was going a-pleasuring, making up for lost time.

George MacBeth and I, though maritally separated, were still united by our love of rambling old houses. In the spring of 1985, my horizons had spread northwards to Caithness where we had just bought a shooting lodge and a loch in the northernmost tip of Scotland. And they had also spread west, to Bristol, where I had gone to sit, for the second time, for my picture by Duff-Scott. I loved the idea of both of them: of Loch Dhu Lodge, all alone on its grouse moor, with its ease and elegance behind its storm doors, standing like a solitary beacon, like a smaller version of St Pancras station dropped down in the middle of nowhere; and of the painter re-creating around him a world of his own. And here, at last, it seemed, was the person I had been dreaming of ever since my early days. For once I didn't have to add any skills or graces to the memory that he left. They were all there, and I was in love with Robbie Duff-Scott, obsessed by him, while he, at least, was obsessed by his painting of me.

Several times during the course of the year I travelled, *en entourage*, to Loch Dhu Lodge. It must be one of the most inaccessible houses in Britain, by road, but imagine my delight on discovering that the unmanned station of Altnabreac is only half a mile from its door. Though the views by road are lovely, with the heather and the lochs, the forty-five minutes of dirt road from Westerdale fill me with dread. I no longer drive myself, but I hate slow driving – that feeling of living with the brakes on. Not so the Highland Line. Six times a day, trains clatter through either way, from Thurso and Wick to Inverness, and from Inverness to Thurso and Wick. The trains stop at Altnabreac only on request. The first time we did this, there was deep snow, which had just been cleared enough to open the roads, but not enough to give access to Halkirk or any of the villages where provisions might be bought. The train that had brought us and dropped us at the lonely station was the only link with the outside world. As the time drew near for the five o'clock to Inverness to pass through, we waded through the snow to the one existing platform, where only the half-covered traces of our own footprints showed any sign of human occupation. I had been told to hold my arm out as for a bus, and it was truly gratifying to see the engine slow and the whole train halt for us. There is even a stepped box that the guard runs round and puts at the entrance so that one may board the carriage with more ease.

At other, less drastic, times of the year, when Loch Dhu is not snowbound, the house comes into its own, with its many views of the loch, and the circling lapwings, and, on clear days, the purple pyramid of the mountain of Morvan on the far side. Although the house rambles and kaleidoscopes at times into sequences of kitchens and larders downstairs, linen rooms and staff bedrooms upstairs, it quickly warms up with the fires and stoves, and when these prove insufficient a flick of the generator switch provides enough electricity to flood the house with light and the rooms with fan heaters. Without the generator, on the long summer nights that darken only well towards midnight, it is a place of wind-up gramophones and candlelight.

It was built, as a hunting lodge, in 1898, with a tower at one end and a turret at the other, and the stone of the house and the coloured beaver-tail slates of the roof stand out for miles around in every direction, the only human landmark in a barren landscape, canopied with heather and bog cotton and inhabited only by grouse and deer. What more can I say? The waters of Loch Dubh (notice the perverse, different, spelling) are so cold that to swim in them is torture, but we do. The trout in the loch are so delicious that it is worth inviting someone up just to stand on the edge and fish for them endlessly, and the walks, though superficially enticing, can suck one into quagmires that are literally waist-deep. Lastly, there are rainbows almost every day, and a sweetness in the air that gives the whole place a magical quality. It is my favourite house. Were it not for my restlessness, I might actually live there.

As it is, the trains quicken, and the plot thickens, and Loch Dhu remains with its spectral halo beckoning in the far north of my mind under the domain of the Lord of the Isles.

I had become so enamoured of my painter that I found myself almost incapable of speech in his presence. On our rare meetings over the first year, I found the emotional strain of seeing him so overwhelming that I kept falling into nervous sleeping fits. Since these would occur during dinners, lunches and conversations, it gave little hint to my would-be suitor that I found any pleasure in his company. His painting kept us together. The modern Magdalen was completed and duly hung in Norfolk, and it seemed to give back to me the confidence of a proper living person.

The painter became an indispensable part of my life. In the spring of 1986 we went as a family to Italy, and Robbie came too. It rained continually, the old villa flooded and the holiday was dogged by disaster. But still our friendship grew, with the almost indecent speed of a desert flower, starved and then drenched by a sudden storm. Robbie had the effect on me of a ski slope and a longed-for burst of daring. I was not exactly pure as the driven snow, so, despite having decided to remain single and footloose for the rest of my born days, I found myself, instead, planning a shared future of volcanic proportions. I was dreaming again, and loving it. I was in love.

Meanwhile, the summer came, and was spent in a small village over the Gulf of Levanto in a hill parish of Enrico the railwayman's home town. In between, I had been to Brazil and Miami, Scotland and France, but no matter where I went, I was besotted.

In the autumn of 1986 I gave in to the flood of my totally novel emotions that were all I seemed to eat, sleep or dream. Robbie lived and painted in a beautiful Victorian Billiard Room in Clifton, Bristol. I had been commuting almost daily from Magdalen Road, Norfolk, to London, Liverpool Street, and then to Bristol Temple Meads. Much as I loved the train, I begrudged the hours taken from Robbie's company. So I moved to Bristol, complete with my nanny, my son and Iseult, who was already at a boarding school near by and had been for two years. We had decided to move to Italy together the following spring. Bristol was an interim arrangement. I was so excited about my life that even Bristol seemed exotic to me, and I withdrew from circulation for a season while I reminted my myths.

11

Venetian hours

To cross over the causeway into Venice has all the sensual thrill of love with the foreknowledge of gratification. The carriages glide over the waters of the lagoon with buoys and seagulls bobbing either side. The smoke and factories of the mainland telescope away, and the domed skyline of the massed islands gets nearer. The terminus of Santa Lucia is squat and dull and utilitarian. The causeway stretches across the lagoon like a solitary finger reaching out from modern times to the timeless jewel of the city. It is the one solid link with the outside world. It has grime under the fingernail that touches the wide steps to the water. It reaches so far and no further. Everywhere else is linked by footpath or canal. The *vaporetti*, the water taxis and the gondolas wait outside the station. The Orient Express goes to Venice, stops at Venice, and once went on to Istanbul, where they built the Pera Palas Hotel to accommodate its passengers. Now it simply stops at Venice, and sometimes it seems that the world has stopped there, preserved for ever like a live scarab in amber. One day, soon, I too shall stop there, and make it my base, dropping my roots down into its newly cleansed waters together with the wooden stakes that are the pilings for the palaces that have stabbed all ugliness through the heart.

There is nothing cloying about its splendour. The canals offset its wealth; sweetmeats are enhanced by water. Venice has no rivals, no peers, no cars and no eyesores. The list of what it does possess is so great that I hesitate even to begin it – suffice it to say that its charms are so legion that millions of tourists and millions of mosquitoes every year cannot decrease them. The silence of the small Venetian canals is unique and wonderful. The city fills one with awe to such an

132

extent that even to leave it is memorable, such is the pleasure of knowing that it exists.

I went there when I was seventeen, and was overwhelmed. My Venezuelan husband led me from the station to the main freight sidings of the railway, and then lay down on a metal bench and fell asleep for the remainder of our visit. He had, to be fair, already seen St Mark's Square two years before, after the flood, when it was crossed by duckboards and the whole of Venice was disrupted by the recent damage. He also had, to be fair, the type of hangover that rendered him catatonic to the world and made him vow, every time they occurred (which was once a fortnight), to give up drinking for ever more. With his sense of eternity thus tarnished by his own endeavours, he showed no interest whatsoever in either seeing, or showing me, the undying beauties of Venice.

I wandered alone through the mass of alleyways, crossing and recrossing the arched stone bridges, lost in the intricate brocade of the streets, not knowing where I was, or if I could ever get back to where I came from, and, for the first time since my marriage, not caring. During my two years on the continent, the two years that I euphemistically refer to as my extended honeymoon, that day was the nearest I came to deserting the man I had married. Criss-crossing the narrow stone streets behind the Doge's Palace, I stumbled upon several churches, but kept finding myself at one in particular: a Gothic construction dedicated to the Saints John and Paul. Eventually, I succumbed, and went in and sat down, staying for a long time under the paintings and tombs and statues, feeling in every sense unworthy. Unworthy for the world and unworthy of this beautiful place I had come to.

There was a silent traffic of old women curtseying to the altar, crossing themselves in an almost cursory obeisance and then getting down to the business of the morning: the lighting of the thin wax candles for everyone whom they missed, or remembered, who had died. Occasionally, when the church cleared, an elderly widow would look round anxiously to me, sitting bowed near the front of the church, to see if I had noticed her non-payment of her tapers. Sometimes one coin would clink into the payment box, and an entire handful of candles would be taken and then lit with whispered endearments to friends and family, all deceased, but all believed to be acutely aware of, and almost waiting for, the wax offerings. The women who did this didn't look mean at all, just poor and conscience-stricken, torn between offending a hard Church, a forgiving God and a host of jealous relations who relied on the light of these candles to brighten the dullness of their days in the back stalls of the heavenly choir. Some of the women spoke for a very long time over their candles, and although their lisping Venetian dialect was hard to follow, they seemed to be carrying on monologues of a personal and often trivial nature, updating their dead mothers and cousins with all their latest acquisitions, alterations and goings on.

When the church was entirely empty I joined the candle shuffle and bought a wax candle which I lit and placed on the tiered, spiked tray, dedicating it, as I did so, to the dead part of myself. Then I left, walking, and later running, appalled at my presumption. For years afterwards I felt a form of guilt for my blasphemous self-concern.

In 1985 I was older, if not wiser, and spent a couple of weeks so blissful that the edges of my memories all blur into a handful of moments, a half-remembered euphoria. Just as some bad memories are too difficult to deal with and get reshaped or destroyed in one's head, so some truly wonderful memories suffer the same process. Happiness and danger, daring, pride, fear and dozens of other emotions remain, but bliss and a certain kind of shame are often erased from memory. I can recall sitting on a wall overlooking the Redentore, and a meal on Giudecca in a restaurant with only three tables and geraniums trailing down from its terrace to the canal, and the feel of the late summer air on my face, crossing water, some colours, some smells, some cats, and that is about all. There was a freak plague of mosquitoes which had closed the airport the week before, and now came in such force that they formed small black clouds over the islands. These were sprayed by emergency government forces, and there were piles of dead mosquitoes, inches deep, lining every window sill and wall.

I went to the beach at the Lido and sat on the sand looking, for once, not out to sea but across the beach itself with its striped day-beds and lounging tourists catching the last summer sun. In 1928 Harry Crosby, one of my more recent heroes, had come here after a throat operation and used to lie out on the sand with his uncommonly dark tan, his Gatsbyesque looks and ways, and the sun tattooed on his back and on the sole of his right foot.

The Lido beach in 1985 could not have looked more proper, and yet I scanned it closely for any signs of wild sex or sudden lust, intrigued by the story that Harry Crosby and his suicide-pact lover Josephine Bigelow had met on the beach, each in their bathing gear, and made love then and there on the sand. Would a girl on her own in a gold bathing dress be rogered by a stranger on the sand nowadays? Times have changed, obviously. The tourists in the bed-chairs and deck-chairs showed no signs of passions roused, and I returned, disappointed as a voyeur but still amused by history, to the lulling properties of the linked islands.

There were other times in Venice, snatched visits that were always superb, and so always had a foot in the well of oblivion inside my head. However, the journey that I remember best is not by any means the most glamorous one, although it was definitely the most bizarre.

I had a numbered couchette ticket through to London, and when I boarded the train at Santa Lucia I made my way straight to my seat, only to find that the compartment I was meant to be in was locked, apparently from the inside.

I knocked and tapped and called, and yet received no answer. Thus I was standing in the corridor as we crossed the causeway over the lagoon. The train was fairly dull. It was October, so the tourist season, which lasts, in Europe, from February 15 to the last week of January, was still in full swing but by no means at its peak. Eventually I took an empty seat in a neighbouring compartment and sat back to muse, with a book in my lap to ward off interruption. (A book is quite good for this, but not infallible. There will always be those who will want to know if it is a good book

and whether it is to be recommended; or those who happen
to have read that particular book, or, more often, one like it,
and are very interested in relating the plot, or lack of it, to
you.)

After about an hour had passed, taking with it a great deal
of modernised Veneto and light industrial Brescia, the door
to my rightful compartment was opened. Armed with my
black crocodile suitcase, I jumped up and waited while the
ticket collector opened the door with a pass key like the tool
used to remove the hub caps from car wheels. He then
ushered me inside and demanded my ticket, which I gave
him. By the window, a big, burly, tattooed, morose-looking
man was glowering at the space between his powerful knees
as though pondering whose head to insert there, and when to
crush it. I hovered by the ticket man, waiting for a moment
to dive back out as nimbly as I had dived in. He, however,
had other ideas, and pointed out to me my allotted seat,
opposite the ageing, bullet-headed Mr Universe. My pre-
liminary unintelligible mumbles of proposed decampment
were waved aside. My ticket was clipped, the next ticket
demanded, and my suitcase lifted up on to the rack directly
over the head of the man with the nutcracker knees. As the
collector read his ticket, studying it as though it were the last
instalment of a popular novelette, the owner of the ticket
broke out into a diatribe of abuse in broad cockney
English.

'Bloody Italians. I hate Italians! What's he reading on my
ticket? Probably can't read. Half of them can't. Can't even
bloody talk English. We should have bombed them all while
we had the chance.'

Having got all this off his extremely hairy chest, he glared
across at me, as though defying me to disagree, speak Italian
or otherwise antagonise him. Intuitively, I felt that it was not
the moment to announce that *I* thought the Italians wonderful
and their language well worth learning, so I issued one of my
most noncommittal smiles and reached for my book,
regretting that it was not a coffee-table edition.

The ticket collector finally left, jabbing at the door as he
did so and saying, 'Open, lascia la porta open.'

The tattooes came alive and leapt from their seat. 'Right, mate,' he said.

The other stared.

'Silly bugger!'

Then a two-headed snake, an anchor and a rippling heart slammed the door shut again, locking it firmly from the inside. I continued to read my book, assiduously.

'Hate Eyeties,' he muttered, and continued to mumble and swear out loud for a while, before asking, 'Hey, you, where are you going?'

'London. I'm going to London.'

'Well, thank God for that, I thought you might be a bleeding frog or something.'

I smiled again, the same oil-on-troubled-waters and don't-blame-me-I'm-an-idiot smile that I had found so useful in the past.

'I've been on this train two months,' he said. 'Can't wait to get off it; get a pint of decent beer.'

Since the train had started at Venice, he couldn't possibly have been on it for two months, but he didn't look as if he wanted to have this pointed out to him, and he seemed to actually need to talk. Whether he really needed to or not, he was going to, and he did. At first I scarcely listened, then gradually he dragged me into his monologue. All the way from Brescia to Victoria I listened, hooked, to the unfolding story of his life.

As the train progressed on its course to Milan and Switzerland, Fred, as he turned out to be, gradually dropped his oaths and expletives and his haranguing complaints and moved into the far more poignant and subtle realms of his heart. There was absolutely no subtlety about the way he made the switch. One minute he was criticising Turkish food and comparing it to Yorkshire pudding and gravy; the next, he had ripped open his loosely buttoned shirt and bared his chest, saying, 'I've had open heart surgery, look.'

Sure enough, from his throat to his navel, a long purple scar lay as though in a ditch between the tangled hedgerows of salt and pepper hair that flanked it. What does one say to a half-metre long cicatrice? Or, indeed, to the proud bearer?

Even his voice changed after this demonstration. The rough, potentially violent man gave way to someone whose strength was now broken and who could accept it; and then to someone who had lost something else, and could not accept that.

The two months on a train were true: he had been travelling through Greece and Turkey, Spain, France, Bulgaria, Romania, Holland and most other places one cared to name in Europe. Fred was a lorry-driver, a real long-distance lorry-driver on the Middle East run. All his life had been spent fighting and hauling and driving in and out of adventures. A year before our meeting, he had had a massive heart attack while loading one of his fleet of lorries. And, although he survived, he lost his strength, and a small part of his anger was for that. While he lay in hospital, his wife nursed him, and she also lost her strength there. Meanwhile, and without ever telling him, she had cancer. As he convalesced, she died, and that broke his heart as no coronary or surgery had been able to. Wherever he was in the world, he hated it. He hated Italy because we were in Italy; but really he hated everywhere because he blamed every-where, and most of all he blamed himself. *He* was still alive with his rough ways, while *she*, so he told me, the gentlest of women, had died.

For six months, he had locked himself in their house and drank.

'I drank every day, everything I could tip down my throat until I passed out. Next day, I'd wake up and pick myself out of the sick and go again. I've got friends, good friends, no family, because she couldn't have none, but friends I've done things for because I care about them, and they care about me.

'They came round, they tried to talk to me. I threw them out. All of them. They said, "You'll kill yourself, Fred." Well, God knows I tried, I drank every off-licence in the neighbourhood dry a couple of times over, I reckon. The boys from the business come round. I told them to bugger off. They used to come round, though, and bring me stuff to eat, and I'd tell them, "Get the booze in." Seeing the state I was in, they didn't want to, not after the first few weeks. But

I told them, "You get the bloody booze in or you get your cards." So they did.

'Now and again, when they caught me a bit less out of my tree, they'd say, "You're killing yourself, Fred." But that's the sad thing, I wasn't, because here I am. I've been in pickles you wouldn't believe, and I've never been afraid to hit someone, kill them, if they pushed me. But when it come to killing myself, like right out, I couldn't do it. I goes into the bathroom. Funny isn't it, that you don't think of killing yourself in the lounge? Like not to dirty the carpet, because She wouldn't have liked that. So I goes back into the bathroom and I take the razor and I try to cut my wrists.

'I know it's silly, but it can't be done with a Bic razor. There I was, hammering away with this little plastic thing. After a bit, I had to laugh. Well, you have to laugh. I broke three, and then I sat down on the edge of the bath and I had a good laugh and I had a good cry.

'The Missus always used to tell me I was hopeless carving anything. I was away weeks at a time, eating here, eating there: a packet of sandwiches, a tin of soup, a transport caff. It wasn't often I sat down in front of a joint, so how was I going to carve it? We made our money. She done the paperwork, I done the business, rode with the lads, kept up the standards; out and back to Saudi Arabia every month, deliver the goods, to some Ali Pasha geezer out there, all peculiar things for them Sultan buggers. Gaw, they'd buy a dozen pianos, four dozen inlaid sewing tables. Hampers and half a ton of blackcurrant syrup.

'Well, what with all my gallivanting I never had much experience with a joint, but once we made our money, we had a lovely house and every Sunday a huge piece of sirloin. I spent a bit of time trying to get the hang of the carving, but the Missus said, "Don't worry, Fred, if you could manage the meat you wouldn't be the man I married." So she done all that. She was used to my not being there and wore the trousers a bit.

'So there I was with a bleeding safety razor scratching away at my wrists like a toy violin. She would have laughed, so I did. Then I thought about how she died and never complained and never said, so as to protect me, and I started to cry. Must have cried for the next couple of months.

'I couldn't say I lived like a pig, because pigs have their habits and I'd lost mine, but I wallowed in such filth I can't believe it now. I mean, a lorry-driver, a real lorry-driver, has to keep everything in order. Take your cab: you've got to have your papers, your stove, billy, food, spanners, and all that, right where you can reach your hand out and find them. There's no point telling some Turkish soldier who thinks he's bleeding Ali Pasha and knows he can have you, "Oh, just a tick and I'll look for them." It's like a discipline. Like being a soldier. You go on parade with a dirty belt and you're in trouble. You go on a run with a dirty anything and you're going to break down and wind up served up as the little greasy bits in some heathen meatball.'

Here, Fred looked across at me and, seeing me doubt his example, he added, 'I'm not exaggerating. Me and my boys, we never stop in Yugoslavia. Not ever, we go straight through, it takes nineteen hours foot on the accelerator and only slow down at the police blocks marked on the map. My map. I don't let the boys stop there, and if they do, they're out. Because I don't want the job of going to their wives, what I know, and saying, "Sorry, Kate, your Jim's gone missing." And you can't even say he's gone missing and they found the lorry somewhere down Zagreb because the whole bleeding lorry disappears with him. It does, they don't leave you a nut or a bolt to identify it by, it just goes into the fourth dimension, and what they can't use they put in them bleeding meatballs again.

'I worked all my life building up that business, built it up from nothing. And now? I wish I had some of the time back that I spent out on the road, staring out at the road, back again, so I could just spend it with the Missus. I thought, here I am, me Fred, getting rich, not quick, but quick enough to make a lot of money. I thought, I'll make a packet, and then we'll retire, get a little place somewhere, make a garden. We didn't have no plans to travel, not with the line I'd been in, I'd seen a bit too much tarmac already, and the Missus used to come along, twice a year, to keep me company. How can you know? How can you know that it won't last? You think if you love someone that's enough, you don't realise you could lose them.

'You don't, do you?'

I shook my head in sad agreement.

'No,' I said.

He looked at me, a flicker of his old aggression surfacing in his eyes, embarrassed suddenly to have talked so much to a stranger.

'What's your name then?' he asked, almost suspiciously. I told him, and he nodded, happier, and reassured. He thought for a moment and then continued, weaving my own name into his sentences as often as he could for the next few minutes as though, by doing so, he could feel he knew me better.

'The thing is, Lisa, I never give her enough attention. I loved her, bought her presents, and I'm a rough man but I was kind to her in bed, kind to her at home. But what is kindness from me compared to what she was, Lisa?'

He shook his head and smiled.

'If you could have seen her, Lisa. What a face! Not pretty, not the kind to make a man turn round, not like yours, Lisa, not like that, but what a lovely face she had . . . No point saying, is there, Lisa, no point trying to show you something that I couldn't even see myself. Not that I didn't love her, but I ought to have loved her more.

'I'd come back from the depot sometimes, and she'd be having one of her bad days, you know, when nothing's quite right . . . she used to look bloody lovely when she was cross.

'We had one sod with us for years, we used to call him "the Captain". You can tell what sort of a character he had when I say that he got chucked out of the Rhodesian police force for being too brutal. A right little Hitler, he was. Always wore his shorts, knee-length khaki shorts, and a safari hat, and he carried a rawhide whip. He looked pretty silly at Felixtowe docks each month, checking his load, but nobody messed with him because he was like the devil in there. The Captain used to come down the depot as gentle as a lamb when the Missus was running things, if I was away, like. I sometimes thought that if he had broken the rules, which he wouldn't dare, but if he had, and he'd stopped in Yugoslavia, it wouldn't be him what wound up in the meat-balls.

'Then we've got this other geezer, "Baked Beans" we call him, because that's all he eats, tins of Heinz baked beans, he spoons them out cold from the tin, every twenty minutes while he's driving he spoons himself out another gobful. You see him setting off and it looks like he's going off to set up a boy scout outing. Twenty open tins of cold beans lined up beside him. He never eats another thing. He's more scared of eating a meatball than landing up inside one.'

And so the night wore on, filled with talk of 'the Missus' and the Middle East Run. Fred told me of smuggling dead bodies (for the best of reasons) wrapped in black rubbish bags and hidden in the back of his refrigerated container lorry. He told me of the bribery, which was consistent, and stretched from England to the Middle East, and he told me of his times in prison – in Turkey and Yugoslavia, and how he got out, and how he got fellow lorry-drivers out, and how there was a hierarchy like bandits of old with their own laws and their own punishments for those who broke them. Anyone caught pilfering from another man's lorry had his arm broken. Anyone caught pilfering twice had his head bashed in.

He described the solitude of the long-distance driver, and how the look of the road can send men mad. He described the different tricks needed to stay awake and driving over long runs. He described the desert landscapes, their colours and their smells.

For dinner, we shared our food, and drank wine and brandy while discussing the merits and demerits of English fare. Despite the first impression that he gave me of hating all things foreign with a kind of ignorant, self-righteous rage, he turned out to have a great sensibility for the Mediterranean, particularly for Turkey, which he knew best. He also spoke a smattering of all the languages that he needed on route from England to Jeddah. Well into the night, when the train had stopped, for no apparent reason, at Basel, he began to rage at the delay that was putting precious minutes between him and his pint of decent beer. Then, mid-sentence, he stopped and smiled.

'You might think I'm an angry man. But I'm not. I used to have it in me, I used to go spare over little things, but all the months on the road, just thinking and talking, got rid of that. I think every time I changed my tyres I chucked out some of my aggro with the old ones. It's only since I done my heart in that I get angry any more, and it's because I don't understand why she died. One thing I've had rattling around on these bloody trains for the last two months, is that I can see that I might come to accept it, one day, not yet. I couldn't yet, but she wouldn't want me to be lying on her carpet in a mess, and she'd want some flowers on her grave, and me to be a man, not an animal. Sometimes, though, I just can't help the temper, I feel like I've got a ginger-beer plant stuck in my brain.'

Our beds had been made up a long time since by a cowed ticket collector, who entered our compartment warily, as though expecting to be sprung on by a wild beast. He was visibly surprised by the change that had come over Fred, and he even looked him over slyly as he was pulling out the couchettes to make sure that he was the same person. There was, even he could see, no doubt about it, for although he hadn't seen the immense scar, the tattooes were enough to identify Fred at fifty paces.

Nothing seemed to be happening, apart from some sporadic calling and workmen walking up and down the dimly lit platform, talking about brakes and other technicalities.

'I expect you're tired,' Fred announced. 'You'd better turn in.'

Whereupon he rose from the seat beside me, which was the only seat left in the converted sleeping carriage, and began to rummage in his small travelling bag for his toothbrush, paste, and a comb for his balding hair.

I hadn't felt tired until he mentioned it, but by the time he returned I was already in bed and half-asleep. He lay down on the berth opposite and down from me, and lay very still, staring up at the blue glow of the night-light on the ceiling.

'You asleep?' he asked, after a while, and then, without waiting for a reply, he went on.

'Here's the first time I ever got into trouble with the law . . . I was twenty-six, I was working hard and minding my own business, when I had to spend some time in England, at the docks waiting to be cleared by Customs.'

For over an hour he told me, whispering now, in deference to the night, how he had blocked an entire Customs dock for a week in retaliation for the rudeness of a guard.

'I nearly went bust over that, nearly, but not quite, and it was worth it just to teach them a lesson. I've never been able to go through those particular docks again, they'd hold me up from now till eternity if I even tried it. So I shifted my business, and I've lost a lot of money over the years because of that. But it was worth it. How often does a little man get a chance to put his point across to a whole organisation?

'I had a wicked temper in those days, for stuff like that, mind you; for that sort of people. I used to have the temper of someone in the right, pig-headed, mind, but in the right.

'I don't know now, I go for little things. If I hadn't spent these two months thinking on the train, I might have been like them, with the mentality of a bleeding Customs officer.'

Fred became silent again, gazing drowsily at the blue light, while I lay back, lulled by the rocking of the train into a fitful sleep.

'Are you asleep?'

It was very early in the morning, somewhere in France. It looked cold and misty through the chink in the window blind, and Fred had drawn his green and red railway blanket up over his grimy string vest.

'No,' I said, feeling very sleepy indeed.

'Did I tell you how I came to be on the trains?'

'No,' I said, hoping that it wouldn't take too long.

'British Rail used to use me. They don't send their goods much by train any more because it's so slow and unreliable, so it all goes by lorry, contracted out to people. It's not the best advertisement for a railway line, is it, if they don't even use it themselves! So I done the business all these years, and one of the blokes there, high up, very high up, was a good friend to me when it came to giving me work when I needed it, so I done him a few good turns in exchange. All work, mind, nothing social. He'd met the Missus a few times, always sent us a card at Christmas and something to go with it. I know him as one of nature's gentlemen, and I knew he respected me for always getting my loads in on time – I'd bust a gut to meet a deadline – but I didn't know he was a friend, not a real friend. He came to see me when I was in hospital, after my operation, and I was touched by that. He came to see me later, at my place. I was too pissed to even notice, effing and blinding on the carpet. He must have called up the depot to say hello, heard about the Missus and come round.

'Next thing I know, he's come back, and he gives me a railway ticket for two months, anywhere in Europe, any train I like, first class. He handed it to me, and he didn't even start to tackle the "Fred, you're killing yourself" bit. No, he says, "Your wife was always very kind to me, Fred, this is the least I can do for her now she's gone."

'Just that. It stopped me from wallowing. Got me out of the house. I reckon it saved my life, that, and the trains, and sitting in them, thinking and remembering and seeing other poor sods who never even had a Missus to lose in the first place. It's not the same as being high up behind the wheel, of course, but I can't drive any more, doctor's orders, and I couldn't bear to be driven. I used to be like the King of the Jeddah Highway, I couldn't sit beside someone else now, like a mattress in the passenger seat. Not Fred! I would never have thought of a train, never used them myself. They've kept me going, over the worst. I'll never get over it all, I wouldn't ever want to. I don't want no birds, no little woman at home. I had my little woman and that's it, and damned lucky too.

'I didn't get off the train, much. I mostly slept on them. I feel easier in myself when I stay on. I could have gone to some great hotels mind, good food, drinks, but it don't mean nothing when your heart won't mend. I must be getting better, because I can't wait for a decent beer. I'm going to have one right at Victoria station, the first since August.'

The train rolled along its route through the flat lands of France on the way to Calais. The willows and fields and scattered, shuttered farmsteads were all doused in fog. It was a thin, watery fog, like the heavy mist that sits almost continually over the Norfolk Fens. Having thoroughly woken me, Fred now seemed lost in his own mists of English beer, lying as if drugged by their prospective fumes. I watched the chill strip-cartoon flashing past my window for a while and then fell into a new comfortable sleep that lasted until the loud dinner bell announced the small breakfast trolley to be at our door.

Over a meal of coffee and ham rolls (Fred hated foreign cheese) we made a date to have a beer together at Victoria station on arrival. I had just agreed to this (one of the few beers I have ever drunk, since it is my least favourite drink with the exception of Fernet Branca), when Fred began to pull at his buttons again. He had a way of appearing to rip open his shirt without causing any damage to the sewing, also of raising his vest in the same gesture, so that it had a real sweep to it. One had the impression that he had bared his chest many times in the past, but whether to show his scar, or, less recently, his strength, one didn't know. However, this time it was definitely the scar that was on display.

I have never liked scars, or, rather, I dislike them. I feel squeamish about them, and, since my own abdomen looks like the street plan for an ill-designed city, criss-crossed by the tracks of many operations, I really have no desire to see other people's. However many stitches there are in a rugby wound or appendix cut, I'm just not interested. Thus, the sight of Fred's sawn-open and restitched thorax was utterly distasteful to me as I chewed my ham roll.

'It's a wicked scar, isn't it!' he announced proudly. I agreed without looking, but still aware of its presence leaning over my coffee cup and crumbs.

'It's disgusting, really, to think of all those people, girls, men, dipping their hands inside you up to the elbow in gunge. It's intimate. What's that thing they do to deer when they kill them, plunging their hands in guts and blood?'

I pretended not to know. I had given up on the ham roll now, and was concentrating just on trying to keep down what had gone before.

'Go on, when they go in right up to the armpit in entrails, you know.'

'Gralloching,' I said.

'Grackling, right, well, it didn't ought to be allowed really. I mean, I don't want anyone to know me that well. It's like being a bloody poofter.'

The train had slowed and passed through Calais Ville; within minutes we would be at Calais Maritime, and it would be time for the ferry. Fred looked morosely out at the receding grey.

'You don't like scars, do you.'

'No,' I said, apologetically.

'Me neither,' he said, and the train jolted to a halt, adding great finality to his confession.

12

Love-letters from the train

Milan to Genoa
August 1987

Dear Robbie,

... Even the train seems strange, and my veil is no
protection. I keep it on because it is a present from Venice, a
transparent carnival hat that cannot mask the numbness of
your departure. It is night-time at Milan Central, and the
train is already nearly full of people elbowing their way
along the corridors, oblivious of Mussolini's grandiose
legacy. I am glad to leave the grey city; sorry to leave the
invisible wake of your plane somewhere on the outskirts of
Italy's industrial wasteland.

If there are to be any seats, they will always be in the very
first carriage. I know this, but have ignored it, hoping against
hope for an entire compartment in which to entomb the
nothingness I feel without you. My suitcase is heavy and my
feeling of approaching depression heavier. All around me,
strains of English filter through. Many of the people who
pass me have come from the airport, arriving as you left. I
feel half-tempted to fall into conversation, to explain that my
love has gone away and I must travel back to Liguria alone
now. But I let them pass, until I find, at last, an empty place,
for six, disguised by dim light. I heave my luggage on to the
rack and remove my hat, feeling a faint sense of betrayal in
so doing. Its black plumes are like a magnet.

The train continues to fill. I miss you. I have six hours of
travel ahead, like six hours of a wake. (The Mars bar in my
handbag has melted.) The train pulls silently along the
platform. I prepare to feel tragic, adjusting myself on the
brown vinyl to do so. The emptiness beside me is due, I now

148

realise, entirely to the absence of any light. You have gone to a funeral; I have stayed to go home and wind up the summer. The stillness of Venice is still in my hair. We have decided to settle there. Plans gel like the perfect hold of so many television ads. I miss you, but for once there is nothing tragic in your leaving beyond the dazed sadness of parted lovers.

I sit in solitary state, daydreaming of the lapis lazuli you love. Every day I can wake up, and, rising on one elbow, see the lapis lazuli of the gulf of Levanto and feel secure in its small waves fringing the hem of my premeditated passion. Without you, I would go over the precipice. If I drink three bottles of spumante I will also go over the precipice because the path to Raguggia is dark and dangerous. At several points there are drops of over a hundred feet. There are marks over the small bridge where the Irishman has wrenched away the path with his falling. Beer and bravado have rechristened him the pathbreaker. Three days ago he was found nearly drowned in a pool of his own sweat on a train to Brescia. Even Paddie, the gold filigree of our cloth, has gone, flown back to London to pour beer on the troubled waters of miscreant computers.

Raguggia is a synonym for inaccessability. Every day, for months, we have trekked through its vineyard along the winding track that dies at its door. The moon has become crucial, not because of any Cancerian elements, but merely because every two weeks out of four it lights the precipitous path that leads us home: when there is a full moon there are no bruises.

The passengers are double stacked in the corridor, and, as though by some prearranged signal, five of them storm the darkness of my compartment. One by one, they look at me with misgiving, as though remembering a collective French lesson when they heard, 'Why does the sun never set on the British Empire? Because God doesn't trust an Englishman in the dark.' Or an Englishwoman; and why isn't the light on? One by one they fiddle with the switch over the door, and one by one they retire into the twilight of their seats.

Every morning I will watch the morning glories flower on the terrace over the sea. I planted the seeds and coaxed the

149

spindly stems to twist and spiral in the excessive heat and relative drought of that verandah. The sight of each new blue flower gives me a physical pleasure; when there are no azure trumpets on display I feel a sense of failure and inadequacy, as though the day were incomplete, half its hours truncated, its air removed. As the train grinds through the darkness, I think about the morning glories, with their thin flowers more ephemeral than butterflies, lasting only a few hours and then dying before midday. They too are shades of lapis lazuli, shades of you.

My journey finishes off the evening and drags through the night. There are no connections. My choices seem to have whittled themselves down to arriving at Levanto at two a.m. and sleeping on the beach with my luggage and the mosquitoes, or hoping that Fernando has returned from Finland. I phone from Genova Principe, fighting off drunkards as I do so. Fernando replies, and I am saved from the insects, and the indignity of being 'caught' on the beach. In Levanto, I am a respectable person, a figure of some renown, poised and elegant in the Café Roma. There is an air of mystery around us; we have been adopted, accepted in our eccentricity, and the town has closed a little to enclose us, protectively, like the sides of an oyster shell around a strange-coloured pearl.

So I make my way from Genova Principe, which is both a great station and a great circus of human dregs, to Fernando's flat in its turret of a castellated mansion on a hill overlooking the port. The taxi winds up the road, cork-screwing through dubious streets to what he obviously finds a dubious destination. I have told the driver that it is near the Jesuit seminary, but that, it seems, is no recommendation. After I leave the taxi there are hundreds of steep stone steps through half-ruined terrace gardens. Were it not nearly midnight, I would succumb to my gardener's urge and pull some of the goose-grass off the roses.

The route from Genova Principe is my route. I do not own it, but I feel as though I do. Once it led only as far as Sestri Levante, but in the last two years, by a process of osmosis, I have moved along the track to Levanto. I have incorporated all the extra names from Deiva Marina to Bonossola into my vocabulary, and each small station has become as familiar to me as the names of my own children. Occasionally I confuse one with another, but this seems like a natural mistake, and, again, one that I make with the names of my young heirs. Beyond Levanto there are five more stations, the Cinque Terre, and these too have become a familiar part of my litany. I always pass them with pleasure, and, like so many places, I know them best from the rails . . .

. . .

Florence to Siena
September 1987

Dear Robbie,
. . . Between the trips, and the night wanderings, and the meanderings, I return to Legnaro, to Liguria and Raguggia. Gradually the bare house is furnished and draped and filled with books, pictures, china and bric-à-brac, all carried from London, Victoria, by courtesy of British Rail and its European counterparts. From Levanto station, the massive trunks are hauled to Legnaro by truck, or, with the smaller ones, in the convertible back seat of the Legnaro school taxi-cum-private car. From there, the carriage of chattels degenerates into the stations of a ludicrous cross, dragging and heaving and lugging things to Raguggia. There are many pairs of unwilling hands to help, and by the end of the first month anyone arriving after the perilous crossing of brooks and vineyards would find a cluttered den, locked in its very private valley. My floating stock of trunks came out of the railway depots and borrowed cantinas, and went to Raguggia. A new batch was bought specially, and by pilfering the castle in Norfolk which had been my base until then, at least for my more cumbersome treasures, Raguggia began to have a settled air about it. So settled, in fact, that I am beginning to look around for somewhere else to decamp to for next year.
  To this end, I studied my little bible, *I treni principali*, and set off for Siena. I have waited a long time to recognise the

charms of Tuscany, partly, I suppose, because it is so widely recognised already. Sensitive English people go to Tuscany, as a matter of course, just as, in the past, impoverished younger sons went into the Church. So many people have extolled its virtues to me, that I have developed a stubborn prejudice against it, just as I do about films. If enough people say to me, 'You must see such and such a film,' I will wait years before I do. (Admittedly, I do eventually sneak into some out of the way cinema and watch the piece in question, but I am, as you know, wary of being in the swim of fashion. Whether this is through a fear of not being able to get out of it, and being condemned to a life of 'in' things and plastic, or whether it is just pig-headedness on my part, I do not know.)

Be that as it may, I, too, have discovered Tuscany. (In Venezuela, when someone does something of the kind, they call it discovering tepid water, or rediscovering America.) I wander in the landscape of the Madonna of the Rocks, entranced. Then, like my vicariously related Granny Mabel on her world cruise, I shut my cabin window with an unspoken 'seen it' and came back to Raguggia. Like so many others, I have come to love Tuscany, but my love lacks passion.

Last year, in the platonic phase of our affair, we sat in the Piazza della Signoria in Florence, with the Uffizi to our left and the fountain to our right and a couple of tumblers of brandy, and you pointed out a tall window like a studio northlight across the square, and chose it for a potential studio. In those days, adding my infatuation on to my natural vagueness, I didn't take in the detail of much that was said to me. Instead, I would spend hours at a time gazing at the picture made by your face, the frame of your dark wavy hair, and your brocade waistcoat, daydreaming of outrageous futures and lost in admiration for your looks (which I found Byronic, though better featured and less fat). Now that you are gone, I make a point, when I visit Florence, of sitting in the same bar in the same square, trying to make of myself an honorary Florentine so that at such time as the easel and canvas move there, I, too, will be prepared . . .

. . .

LOVE-LETTERS FROM THE TRAIN

Dear Robbie,

. . . Have you noticed that the station at Levanto, like many others along the Italian Riviera, is ugly and squat and has little life of its own? The station at Sestri Levante is a dossing place for tramps. It has a permanent collection of some six or seven who add character to its regulation benches each time they grace them, and they grace them every night; but Levanto is bare and functional. Once, the railway line cut right along the coastline: a single track carved and blasted through the rocks. Then, after the First World War, everything expanded and there was no room to widen the line, so the old railways became what are now parts of roads, and the new double tracks were built further away – hence the back to front look of so many Rivieran towns. Hence, also, the rows of modern flats leading up to these bare blocks of stations.

One can ride from anywhere to anywhere along that coast, and between the darknesses of the tunnels there are flashes of prettiness and age clinging on to the very rock-face, tumbling into the sea, and almost any one of them seems like a wonderful place to stop. When one has the more serious business of a holiday in hand, arrangements will have been made, tickets bought to a particular place, and the name of the bit of paper in one's pocket then becomes temporarily appropriated by the holder. One talks of 'my station' or 'my stop'. After glimpses of hill villages afar, and streets and roofs, from the train, the first sight of the outside of one of these stops and the town around it can be a grave disappointment. The panic at having made the wrong choice, and the disappointment, settle grimly with the dust and the flies before even the third suitcase has been wheeled through the stiff glass doors.

At Levanto, the incoming tourists jostle off the train and hurry out, only to rest their cases, or, more often, backpacks, against the huge picture windows, leaning against them themselves like insects driven by a strong wind until another gust can carry them on to the old-world elegance or the kitsch and cornflakes or the camping sites that will and must be both a beginning and an end. Some of the towns, like Lavagna, have kept their stations where they always were, and found a way to double the track *in situ*; they are thus less spoiled, but have the drawback of running down more than the normal quota of pedestrians who cross the railway tracks at the level crossings in town, judging the speed of all trains by the sleepy stopping one they came on. They do not realise that the express trains from Rome and Naples hare along the coast and cannot stop, even for old people, even for young people, even for lovers. Six people were once killed at Lavagna, in one go, and that's the local record. My good friend, the ubiquitous Enrico of Sestri Levante and Levanto both, was a train driver at the time, along the same route. He told me that train drivers are not allowed to stop on pain of prosecution, because, by stopping or even braking an express train, the driver could derail it, or worse, thus causing the loss of hundreds of lives.

A week after the incident at Lavagna, Enrico was driving the Rome Express to Genoa. As he rattled through the tunnels that form such a large part of the Ligurian line, he found himself brooding on the recent incident and wondering what it must have felt like to have seen the front of the train after it stopped and before it got sluiced down, and how it must feel, if it did at all, at the moment of impact. Would the victims know what had hit them? So many tunnels, and then the very long one that leads to Moneglia, and then, out of his morbid thoughts, he saw a dot on the line, coming closer. It was a man. Enrico sounded the whistle, flashed the lights, sounded the whistle, horn, bell, and the man kept grinning like a would-be suicide crouching in the middle of the path of the oncoming train. The man wouldn't move, and Enrico couldn't stop the train, so he ran him down, seeing his smiling face at the last minute. Then came the emergency signals to the next station, permission to stop, and the Rome Express screeched into the small platform and its ashen driver staggered down from the cabin. The incident was described, a shuttle went back, and there was the man, with half his body above the tracks and the other half down a manhole, grinning. The practical joker apologised. He was sorry. Enrico was even sorrier, and he never drove a train again, hence his presence, by shifts and turns, at Sestri Levante station . . .

. . .

Levanto station
October 1987

Dear Robbie,
. . . I already know the temperature of the beer at Levanto – very cold, and anyway not to my taste – and the quality of the wine and the makes of brandy (pronounced, by popular demand, brendy) available. I know the taste and texture of the waxy sweet croissants filled with fatty ham and the never quite fresh doughnuts that bear, when squeezed, a most unfortunate resemblance to a carbuncle, exuding a thick jet of custard. I know the juke-box and its choice of crooning songs and heavy metal, and I know the small snooker table where games can be had for 1000 lire. I even know the pair of elderly men who always dally longer at the station than their trains require so that they can supervise and manipulate the game, gracefully taking a cue from the unsuspecting hands of a player and then destroying the game by breaking every available rule while strutting round the table saying proudly, 'You see, that is how it is done,' and, 'Did you see that? Huh?' And I know the tunes of the *salagiochi*, the inane jingles of the video games that provide a background to everything that takes place at one end of the station. And, maybe, these attractions in themselves do not seem enough to endear this particular station to me, other, perhaps, than it has come to be home and is thus allowed to limbo dance in under the door of more prepossessing places because, like an ugly cousin, it falls under the blanket protection of familiarity.

But there is another reason, stretching far beyond the friendly nods of the luggage department through which several tons of my trunks and cases have been lugged and hauled and docketed. It stretches beyond the waiting taxi drivers (perhaps because they are never available after dark).

It is, in fact, a simple view from the platform, a view up into the hills behind Levanto, scanning round its *frazioni*, or parishes, with the villages of Montale and Lavaggiorosso and Ridarolo clawing hold of their perches of rocks like overgrown eaglets about to fall from their nests. Most prominent, because nearest, of all these tiny medieval villages is Legnaro. And beyond Legnaro, on the Montale side, sitting like a semi-precious stone half-way up the valley with nothing but olive groves and vineyards on either side to link it to either church or village or cemetery, there stands an old, tiered, rambling house entirely and incongruously on its own, and that is Raguggia.

I first saw it from the station, clearly visible, although some ten kilometres by road, only two or three as the crow flies. I had it pointed out to me two years ago, since when I have stood on the same shabby station and pointed it out, first to you, and then to every arriving visitor, each of whom stare up in wonder and admiration for the beautiful landscape around it, little knowing that within twenty minutes they too will be traipsing across the single-lane track in the wake of the pathbreaker.

When night falls (and guests have recovered from their frights and falls), we sit on the top terrace with the wisteria and the bougainvillaea and whatever else has withstood my frequent absences from the watering can and their roots, accompanied only by the sounds of ourselves, and owls, and cicadas. Sometimes there are dances on the terrace, and the villagers say they can see the candles and lamps from Legnaro. Sometimes Daniele comes, from his opera classes in Florence, and when he sings on the terrace at Raguggia they can hear him in Levanto, such are the acoustics of the valley and the power of his voice.

Even when there is no one there but ourselves, there are always lights from the other villages, and what looks like city lights but which are only the lights of Levanto funnelled to a head directly in front of our house and below, far away but each one visible, like so many fireflies in the night. From out of the mass of individual flames, a long glowing line like the luminous dorsal spine of a great fish lies horizontally across the near edge of the town. By day it is scarcely visible with the naked eye, swallowed up by the general mass of buildings around it; but by night it shines out like a backbone of memory guiding strangers through the twin row of lights that mark its tracks, with its heart at the station. The same station that looks so ugly close up by day has a mysterious glow now, and a new importance. It is the last nocturnal landmark before the sea.

Do you know, Robbie, I have never lived at Raguggia on my own? We spent the longest of our many honeymoons there and I have since become accustomed to being surrounded by an entourage of family and friends. I have what amounts to a fear of my own company. Soon the sanest and nicest part of the film world will move into Raguggia with me, and there can be dancing again and drinks on the terrace. Meanwhile, I have a few days ahead of me. I think I shall pass the little house in Legnaro and take Iseult back across the track with me, and maybe Alexander would care to abandon some of his noisier pastimes and listen to Puccini with us.

I feel like the heroine of a great opera, or at least the heroine of a bad play. I have resisted the temptation to travel on. Robbie, my love, with you at your funeral, I feel funereal, but I have turned down the usual temptation of perpetual motion. The taxi curves around the last bend to Legnaro, missing the white dog that lies in the road dicing with death today as it has done for the last eight years, I'm told, and pulling up in front of the bar. I get out and pay. Arrivederci, and good day, good day to the lady at the bar and her mother, and good day to the lady who grows tomatoes and tends the grapes around Raguggia, and good day to the old woman with the big boobs who works so hard but seems to enjoy some private joke and seems always on the verge of sharing it. And good day to the man with the throat operation whose growled replies are all that are heard in the street outside his ravaged stone house from one hour to the next, and good day to the child at the tap.

I have travelled so long that the days of my last journey, which number six, merge into the days and weeks and years stretching back, now only four years, now eleven, now twenty-four and I feel glad that I have stopped 'home' today.

Glad to pick up some of the more usual goings on of a home. I look forward to seeing the children, though they are scarcely that any more. Iseult looks nearly twenty, and has done all year, and Daniel, my nephew, half of a twin, is fifteen.

My fond thoughts for my daughter are soon erased by the news that she has gone to Milan. I am told, on unreliable information, that she may be back in five days, if not seven. Her note tells me that she is sorry just to run off like this, but she has never seen Milan. She had to go, she says, with strangers, whom she forgets to name, because they had a car, and she couldn't wait to take the train.

Along the steep part of the path which you, a weary luggage-bearer, have christened Calvary, I try to reconcile my mind to the loss of my daughter. Is it a loss or a growth? I don't know. I feel unexpectedly calm. It is ten o'clock in the morning, and I am within sight of the fading pink stucco of our house. The grapes are ripe on the latticed trellis overhead, the sun is climbing and the morning glories on the terrace will still be out. It seems that Iseult is overtaking me in age, and that whatever drives her is so strong it will push her down whatever paths she wants to go. She could be lost or raped, but a silly powerful sense of trust in life tells me that she is not. She will see Milan, with Mussolini's great station and all, and she will return neither older nor wiser. I cannot, or will not, believe she is other than reckless and restless and naïve. She will come back, and we will go back in ten days to England, via Amsterdam, on a Dutch train. Meanwhile, I am still thirty-three (the age of Christ), just, for another fortnight, and I am in love and ready to sit down and write letters, lots and lots of letters, about landscapes and matters of the heart . . .

. . .

Viareggio to Levanto
October 1987

Dear Iseult,
. . . The set of Lake Massaciuccoli is filled with the real and imaginary strains of opera. On the Viareggio side of it,

Puccini lived and worked in a small villa at the water's edge in a tiny, semi-feudal parish called Torre del Lago. Now a town has grown in the hinterland of his house. The town is full of streets called Madama Butterfly, Via Tosca, La Bohème and the like. Puccini himself is interred in his villa, in the wall behind the piano that he worked at. The villa is now a museum left exactly as it was when the Maestro died. People come from all over the world by the thousand to visit this shrine, and are allowed in, in batches of ten, to be shown round the exquisite interior and to see the relics of his three loves: good libretti, wild duck and beautiful women.

It is less than fifty years since Puccini's death. In his life-time, he was mobbed by fans and adored and revered. Now his cult grows apace, and the streets subdivide and clone with it, but the view from his villa is unchanged. The green-khaki waters and the clumps of marshes are still full of duck. Even the restaurant built on stilts over the lake itself is still there, and still owned by the same family, and still serving roast duck, although it is true that the restaurant has expanded from the mere cabin that gave it its name.

We sit on the planked terrace, watching the soupy waters slap against its pilings, and eat and drink, safe in the knowledge that Chez Emilio stays open long into the night. Last July, during the Puccini Festival, it served banquets at one in the morning for anyone with the foresight to book. Puccini is like God in Torre del Lago, like the head of a religious cult.

Every time I came to Torre del Lago, the Puccini Festival seemed to be just over or not nearly ready to begin. But finally, after tracking and hunting its timetable, programme, tickets and all, I too waited to cross over an arched, lamplit footbridge to the theatre, where I took my seat for *La Bohème* and was transported by the sweet strains of 'Che gelida manina'.

Until recently, the prospect of an opera would have rendered me semi-comatose with boredom, and if there was any transporting to be done it would have been of the early criminal kind. I always regarded opera and opera-loving as an extraordinary aberration. Mark Twain, the man with an epithet for everything, like a bottle of Victorian universal remedy in human form, said that Wagner was 'not as bad as it sounds'. One dose of the *Ring*, at an early age, during which I had scarcely even been able to sleep, was enough to keep alight a small phosphorescent glow of loathing for everything of that ilk. When opera came on, I switched off; and when friends of mine confessed to a liking for the stuff, I didn't like them any the less, but I lowered my opinion of their taste and intelligence a notch or two as a result. Now I have espoused the cause and love of opera, particularly Italian opera, with such devotion and passion that I feel almost apprehensive at taking up other new interests, lest I become a Savonarola or a Mrs Jellyby.

The little train from Viareggio hummed with snatches of songs. In the compartment next to ours, a man was trying to remember the tune of the theme from *Turandot*, stopping and starting like the train itself as it jogged its way down the few miles from the resort to the musical Mecca of Lake Massaciuccoli. Gradually, the aria carried from carriage to carriage, passing through the thin partition walls with their 'views of Tuscany' in black and white, while the summer Technicolor of real life passed by the windows. The station itself is little more than a stuccoed outpost on the wrong side of the track. When the train emptied and departed, it left a throng of people moving like a throng of guests all invited to the same party. True baritones, tenors and sopranos mixed with the hopeful croaking of true enthusiasts. Our goal was the lakeshore, and the Maestro's house, and the bronze statue by the water of Puccini himself in a turned-up overcoat like a thirties gangster smoking a cigarette. (In his most famous portrait, he is also smoking, although by then he had the throat cancer that was to kill him; so he held it rather than inhaled, on the grounds that the Maestro just wouldn't be the Maestro without a roll of tobacco hanging out of his mouth.)

We waited outside the railings of his villa in sun and rain for the appropriate quota of people to arrive to make up a ten, or even, in winter, a six, because as the custodian points out Italy is a democracy and a majority vote wins. In this land of referendums and elections, where governments fall and rise almost as regularly as the phases of the moon, we elected to spend all the hours we could steal from our own stock of time leaning over the verandah of the restaurant on the lake in the shadow of greatness, with the surrounding mountains on the far side reflected in the muddy waters stirred only by ducks and moorhen and the occasional fish making its own ripples on the surface . . .

.   .   .

Livorno
October 1987

Dear Robbie,
. . . My experience with Livorno has always been fleeting. The first time I went there it was five o'clock in the morning, and I got off a train from the south to be sick. I walked for a while in the chill, misty morning, through the deserted town towards the docks, and then I was sick against a wall. My first reaction on recovering from this unpleasant experience was one of total alarm. Looking at the pavement, up and down the street, I saw a great quantity of vomit which I feared was mine, until I realised that I had chanced upon a favourite retching place. The other parts of the city were sanitarily more acceptable, and my own behaviour was also more civilised, but everywhere was battened and shuttered and cold, and I soon left to warm up on a northbound train. The only other times I have been to Livorno are by mistake, when trying to get to Viareggio and Torre del Lago or Florence, and I have fallen asleep on the journey.
   Do you remember seeing, in the early evening, the extraordinary train leaving the station for Lourdes? You dubbed it the Leper Express, for its invalids, walking-wounded and dying passengers, all accompanied by relatives, and attended by a flock of sisters of mercy. I recall standing on the platform opposite while it prepared to depart, the surreally disturbing sight of the nuns, and any passengers able enough, leaning out of the windows in a line-up of toques and mangled, fevered faces, all staring out, impatient

to be off. The sinister grey train was marked with red crosses.

The journey must be like a nightmare, and at the other end, who knows who will be cured? Those with most faith, it seems, will be the ones who return home, well, or at least eased. The faces that one sees, exposed as through a rent in hospital screens, are the faces of men and women who have played the lottery on their local street corners and who know that only a few can win. Within the lottery of life, they have already lost, and the unwritten rules of chance are playing against them. Under their grimness, this sad awareness shows through, here in the dullness of an eye, there in the stretching of the brow or the wringing of hands.

It is said that the victims of cancer who recover best are those who refuse to believe that they have the disease. Of the others, the fighters stand a chance, and the resigned ones die. Knowing this, that resignation kills, it makes it doubly sad to see the train load up with its wasted human cargo. Bad as it is to watch the Leper Express depart, it must be saddest of all to see it return, with no miracle at the end of the night, and no hope at the end of the tunnel . . .

13

'Why, I do like one or two vices, to be sure'

In the spring of 1987, with both love and Italianitis deeply rooted in my blood, the natural place to have settled would have been Florence. It may come as no surprise to hear that I did not. On the other hand, although I may seem to live as by the random halting of a roulette wheel, in fact it is not so at all. Or, rather, if I do, it is with a great deal of cajoling and cheating and tilting the table so that the wheel will stop and point out the place of my choice. These choices are built like great Renaissance edifices and are as solid as marble; only their foundations are weak. They are not as churches built on sand, but rather altars built on a heap of dreams. It is the strength of the illusion that upholds them. Like Harriette Wilson and her loves, 'I shall not tell how or why' I came to be in Siena; suffice it to say that April 1987 found me there sifting through secluded villas with a view to renting one for the following winter.

I found three splendid, decaying piles, that fitted very handsomely my idea of where the entourage should quarter, and went away to reflect. They were all in the province of Siena and near to the city built on its three hills of pigment. What could be more suitable for a painter than to be within a boarding-house stretch of the burnt and raw siena that go on to his canvas?

The nearest station was called Colle Val d'Elsa, which has the touching idiosyncrasy of being still in use but trainless. To the usual, theoretically strict, but actually lax, timetable of the Italian railways, a bus emerges from inside the station building and wends its way to Poggibonsi. Although it very obviously is a bus, everyone calls it a train. Enquiries about the bus to Poggibonsi will bring no answers relevant to this service. The mere fact of its parking on the railway lines transforms it into a train. From the point of view of a compulsive rail-rider, this poses an interesting conundrum. Am I a train, and if not, will I become one in the eyes of the locals if I take a regular route to Colle Val d'Elsa and back? And are there villagers scattered all over the Sienese hills making engine noises on winter afternoons with the full approval of their neighbours?

On the slow stopping train from Poggibonsi to Florence, I remembered all the details I could of the three villas so that I could relay them later. One, on reflection, seemed so far up a dirt track that visitors could have been excused for planting a flag on arrival and claiming it as theirs. The views were divine, receding into Leonardo's blues. It seemed less like a love nest than somewhere to retire to with a broken heart. Neither did its inherent poetry include any lines about dashing out for a packet of cigarettes or matches, while mundane necessities, like bread and wine and other food-stuffs, would have had to have been airdropped. The only neighbours to speak of were not ones to speak to, since they had long inhabited the cemetery that lay just outside the ancestral gates. Had I been buying, rather than renting, none of these trifling points would have deterred me, but as things were I struck the place of no return off my list. This left a simple choice of two. With my estate-agent duties thus whittled down, I sat back and relaxed, content to leave the choice to my doubly impractical painter.

It was the rush hour at Santa Maria Novella, and the train I was waiting for was one of my favourites, the Rome Express. It would take me to La Spezia, where an orange and beige double-decker would carry me through Monterosso to Levanto again. It looked as though Rome and its aunts and uncles, mothers-in-law, wife, ex-wives, cousins and god-parents were all travelling on the same train, and had all got on first, and were glued to their seats and most of the corridors as well.

Having imagined that villa-hunting would include a great deal of shaking hands and drinking coffee with the owners of the fine places I wanted to rent, I had come dressed accordingly, looking extremely ladylike and well-groomed. This had, in fact, proved quite unnecessary for the cross-country scrambles along unmade roads that had ensued. It also aroused a mixture of jeering and cheering as I clicked my way along the platform looking for that most unlikely of places, an empty seat.

At the far end of this particular grimy iron horse, I spotted not only a free seat but an entire empty compartment. I boarded, and planted my own small flag in the guise of my black suitcase on the rack. On doing so, I noticed some amused, curious faces laughing at me from the corridor, and also a strangely unpleasant smell. Since the general atmosphere for the last five minutes had been heavy with sweat and bananas, the latter was not unduly disturbing; and since Italian youth has a way, *en masse*, of laughing at anything, nor was the former. I was surprised that no one else came in to claim the five remaining seats, but not enough to be deterred from choosing a corner by the window and settling down to my book.

After the doors had all slammed and the wheels had begun to turn through the flaking stuccoed suburbs draped with washing-lines, I discovered why nobody wanted to sit with me. They had seen my travelling companion, who had left what I had thought was my compartment for some reason, but was now on his way back. I was first made aware of his arrival by a mixture of an addition to the smell I had already noticed and a snickering sound from the corridor outside. On looking up, I saw a figure more like a monster than anything I had ever seen. My first reaction was to look away, my second was of pity, and I nodded speechlessly while trying to swallow my distaste. He lumbered in, pushed the door to, and hurled himself down opposite me, removing his broken shoes with one hand and shoving his feet on to the seat beside me. I could never describe the nauseous richness of the smell that hit me, nor the filth that must have been inside the shoes.

Outwardly, or, rather, intrinsically, this man had no physical deformity, and yet he contrived to look and act like a monster. He was not a Quasimodo, he was of the Hammer

165

horror genre, a master of special effects. Thus, his dread-locked hair was matted and full of the most unspeakable rubbish, some of which was scaling down the sides of his cheeks. His face, which could have been Arab in origin but was hardly identifiable, was caked with various layers of general debris, like strata through which pseudo-volcanic eruptions struggled to break through. His eyes were caked, his fingernails were, when not broken, several inches long, every visible orifice of his body that could dribble, did, and his clothes were mere rags tied round with string.

Between stealing glances at his filthy state, and wondering what chain of events could have reduced him to it, I kept catching sight of the corridor youths who were jostling with each other to peer in and then retire amid sounds of loud hilarity, only to return and stand at the door making ape imitations and lumbering like amused orang-utans outside our door. The monster stared through his running dirt, obviously used to such treatment. There was a lot of loud speculation as to how many minutes I would stick it out with him. I terribly wanted to get up and stand in the corridor with the uncouth youths, but something inside me just wouldn't let me rise to my feet, so I continued to read my book as best I could while the heady, noxious fumes filled the air.

He reminded me of my old childhood friend, Garter, who used to sweep the edge of Clapham Common and who was always laughed at for his low intelligence and his rags and his caked filth. He also reminded me, somehow, of Napoleon, my pet turkey vulture in Venezuela, who had broken his leg and had it reset in clumsy splints by me. While the small bone set, Napoleon had had to be chained to a tree to keep him from running around and refracturing his leg. He had spent weeks tearing at the iron chain (he could have torn anything less strong with his beak), steeped in his own excrement, with his beautiful black feathers all torn and caked and his grotesque bare neck, which looked like a grizzled scrotum at the best of times, weighed down with muck.

Every time I buried my mind in the open pages of my book, I managed to conjure up some fleeting similarity between the massive person in front of me and some other derelict character with whom I felt, if not some affinity, then, at least, a kind of respect. There was Cristobál from the Andes, who also had a mass of wild hair and was a tramp and walked for miles every day on his one remaining leg and a long staff. Then there was 'Il Maresciallo', from Sestri Levante, who spent all his pension on sweetmeats and sugar which he submerged into the several litres of white wine that he drank every day and then spilt and dribbled down his front. 'Il Maresciallo' had a humped neck from sleeping slumped on a station bench. There were others, many others from my acquaintanceship with human dregs, but they all had something that I could find to admire in them, and they were, in their own way, romantic. Every time I remembered my first impressions of this collection of unkempt eccentrics, I felt obliged to make the effort to remain in the compart-ment; but every time I saw the monster in front of me again, I merely found in him the most disgusting example of mankind I had ever come across.

At one point, he took my book from me and returned it with grease-marks where his fingers had been.

'Eenglish,' he grunted.

I nodded again.

From a bag that he was carrying, he then drew out a whole cooked chicken. The bag was otherwise full of very dirty laundry, which, in his case, was probably just his other clothes. Water appeared to bear no part in his life. Next, he tore the chicken in two, dropped one half on to the bare floor and proceeded to throw the other half at his face. Once in a while he caught a bite; once in a while he dropped it. The top layer of caked grime came off with the greasy chicken skin, revealing an ingrained layer underneath. There was a madness in the way he ate, as though he were performing a circus trick. Sure enough, a great number of passengers squeezed up to the window to watch. At one point he caught me staring at him, and, picking up the remainder of the carcass from the floor, offered it to me. He seemed genuinely puzzled when I refused, and continued to aim it at his own face with gusto, alternating it with what was left of the first half, as though playing two balls against a wall. His next course was an orange, eaten in the same manner, after the skin had been pulled off with his fingernails.

He tried every few minutes, and when his mouth was fullest, to lure me into a conversation in French. When he spoke, he sounded very much like a member of *Homo sapiens*, and this was more disconcerting than not. I had just got him safely behind metaphorical bars while transporting him out to some hilly area of the Atlas mountains or nearby coastal plain, when he came up with sentences like, 'Où est Cherry White?'

That what he said sounded like nonsense seemed so natural that it was some time before I deciphered this not as, 'Who is Cherry White?' but, 'Where is Terry Waite?' Then, I found the notion of this man reading a newspaper and keeping up with world events so strange that it made me smile. Whereupon he repeated his question repeatedly, and with great insistence, as though he felt that I had some special knowledge of the missing envoy's whereabouts which I was keeping from him.

Having finished his meal, leaving the compartment looking as though the chicken had not only been eaten in it, but had also lived, died and been cooked in there as well, he slid down on his seat to relax. By so doing, he brought his monstrous feet to within inches of my nose. I shied away, banging my head on the glass, and, deciding that not even a sister of mercy of St Jerome himself could have accused me of being either snobbish or unkind, got up to leave. He, however, showed no signs of moving to let me by, as I attempted to rise to my feet, so I decided to wait until the next visitation of curious locals arrived outside the compartment and call for assistance.

Meanwhile, he began to rummage in his loin for something, which he eventually pulled out triumphantly, like a small dead fish. I stared resolutely at the black and white shapes on the page of my book while he played with himself half-heartedly. He seemed very dissatisfied suddenly, and began to mumble things in French. He was still muttering when the train pulled into La Spezia and two naval cadets ventured into the carriage. I don't know which they found most monstrous, the sight of him, the sight of me locked in my corner, or the tremendous stench from his feet. I took the opportunity of their arrival to force my own way out, and stood in the corridor for some minutes wondering what they would do. They remained, cowed and silent, looking with embarrassment at the masturbating monster, and then back, helplessly, at each other.

When he leant over and demanded, 'Où est Cherry White?' they nearly jumped out of their skins. They completely ignored his question, having regained their composure, but there ensued a conversation between them about what language had been spoken and, in the event of it being either French or English, which of them knew most. Having decided that the smaller, thinner of the cadets could say more of the words of 'Sunday, Bloody Sunday' and had sung a few to prove it, the two stood up, as though by some prearranged signal, and bolted through the door. I followed them along the gangway, pushing past smokers and children and seatless passengers as I went. Once over the accordioned link to the next carriage, we all stopped.

'What was that?' one of them asked me. I shook my head, and they shook theirs.

'Cos'era che?' someone else asked. And they began to explain about the ungroomed apeman in the next wagon down, and how he stank. A group of bored youths, mostly in naval uniform and on their way back to their own cage at La Spezia, decided to go and see for themselves. After a while I heard their voices from far away. Everywhere seemed tainted with the smell of dirty clothes and smelly feet. Where were all the hills of Siena now, or the pretty villas, or even the inaccessible one? Where was anyone I knew or could sit by without feeling ashamed?

On arrival, later, at Levanto, I had become, retrospectively, so alarmed by the monster's existence that I ran out of the station and out of the forecourt and down the hill and over the bridge to Enrico of Sestri's house, where I threw myself on his door and his bell like someone escaped from hell. Both he and Rinate, his Austrian wife, are used to my turning up at any hour of the night with bizarre problems, so they showed little surprise now as I rushed past them into their bathroom and proceeded to scrub my face and hands and arms with a hint of frenzy.

Enrico has a theory that it isn't safe to travel alone on the trains if you're a woman. After hearing about my travelling companion from Florence to La Spezia, he told me that people like me finish up with the dirty laundry on the Italian railways, and why was I gallivanting around on my own again, and why didn't I get my head seen to, and why on earth did I want to go to Siena?

The three hills that Siena is built on are literally made of clay, but had they been made of gold, the name would still be mud to the Genovese. It may be centuries since the city states ceased, but the rivalry still runs high. To decamp is treason, tempered, in my case, only by the retention of Raguggia, to which it is known we will return, if only sporadically.

14

Miscellany that leads to Mexico

The delusory spell continues, despite the interludes of squalor. For every mishap there are thousands of miles of contentment, hundreds of days spent reading books and newspapers from cover to cover, writing letters after months and even years of silence, and meeting strangers, and playing games. I have games of chess that are finished and still unfinished all over Europe, and games of Scrabble with my sister on the way to summers in Italy, and card games, for fun or for money, and hundreds of games of Briscola with Iseult, and of Bezique, when I was a child travelling from Leningrad to London, and then, later, of poker dice, with Joanna.

Meetings on trains are as random as the throw of a die. One throw can bring a pair maxim, another a full house or just an uncoordinated batch of people. Travelling seems to lend power to conversation, the knowledge that time is a factor inspiring a temporary telescoping of the faculties and a sharpening of the brain. Thus even those who might over a longer period prove boring and uncongenial develop surreal qualities as conversationalists. Sometimes there is just the one story in them, which a follow-up meeting on terra firma will merely prompt them to tell again, and again, and again. More often there is a secret that can be unfolded only out of context. This can take the form of a revelation, or a confession, or a fabrication, and each one is a part of the tapestry of lives one might never otherwise see, let alone know.

As a child I used to do tapestry with coloured wools on squares of hessian, somewhat ungratefully received presents that arrived by post at Christmas and disappointed one under the tree. I preferred embroidery of the most intricate kind, and sometimes baulked at the monotony of tapestry, especially when the end result was a gaudy bowl of anemones or a sad-eyed spaniel. A colleague of my mother's used to tell me that when one was tired of tapestry one was tired of life. Although subsequently the Bayeux, and the Venetian and Florentine and Flemish versions of the art, have borne this out for me, I do occasionally contrive to settle for a little hemstitch or herringbone in the corridors of trains where I can travel alone, or with friends and family in a group of six, or six plus any number divisible by three, the enforced division of sexually segregated sleeping berths. Ordinary couchettes, for six, are not segregated, nor do they need to be, since even the most puritanical authorities would agree that sexual intercourse is so uncomfortable there that none but the most thwarted lovers would attempt it. Gone are the days when girls woke up on trains wondering whose arm they have wrapped about their naked back. And although sometimes the dice roll in such a way as to accommodate the lustier passions, second-class sex is relegated on the whole to the guard's van and to those best versed in the more difficult positions of the *Kama Sutra.*

If Baudelaire knew that the true travellers are those, and those alone, who set out only for the journey's sake, why can't everyone else? It is always hard to believe or accept that one's likes and dislikes are not shared by those one most loves. To live with someone who loves travelling, in the sense of being in foreign places, but who does not enjoy the journey itself, is, potentially, alarming. I prefer to believe that, gradually, a map of fond memories, composed entirely of journeys, will jigsaw into the brain, grafting a tolerance of delays and inconveniences on to a rootstock of glamour. I hide the more tedious details away, not just from my lover, but from all who travel with me. I haggle and wheedle and bribe so that others may taste the addiction of the trains. On the slow train to Italy, every year, as I ferry the house-parties out to wherever I have pitched my trunks, there are hampers of food: exotic fruits, home-made pies, a cheese board and champagne. I carry flasks of brandy and gin, and the makings of cocktails, and a silver shaker. I spend hours scouring the auctions of East Anglia, buying the best and most beautiful picnic baskets, fitted with Victorian porcelain and silver spirit bottles and cut-glass dishes for special sauces, all to disguise the absence of any restaurant car. When the service returns, I'll be there; meanwhile, standards must be maintained. Some routes still serve meals, but far, far too few.

When I travel alone, with my small black suitcase, I can travel anywhere and my luggage is no inconvenience, just as, when I travel alone with three incredibly heavy leather trunks, they are no inconvenience either, because they are so ludicrously disproportionate to my strength that someone will always come and help. Unfortunately, the price one pays for companionship is the sight of railway staff and fellow travellers merely looking on with pity to see two able-bodied people wrestling with their joint luggage. Thus the painter who is my lover, in between stretching his canvases, is gradually elongating his arms with the accumulated weight of my travelling bags. He himself, while criticising the bulk and number of my cases, is a man constantly armed with a good book to read, and all too rarely a Livre de Poche, or a Penguin, or one of those lightweight tomes which a number of other excellent publishing houses have come up with.

I sometimes pride myself on the fact that my luggage weighs the same whether it is full or empty. The leather of my cases is so thick, and the empty article so cumbersome, that few can tell the difference. Yet, when packed with a couple of pairs of old riding boots and three of the painter's art or architectural books (with full colour plates), they do, definitely, reach hernia level. I believe that when carrying very heavy luggage the art of gaining assistance from anyone other than the odd and exceedingly rare Samaritan, who will undertake any kind of alien baggage, is to bear the thing as though, appearances to the contrary, it were very light. Particularly in the Mediterranean, but elsewhere as well, it disturbs healthy males to see an attractive female swinging what should be a heavy suitcase. If by labouring and straining with the problem help fails to be prompted by pity, by carrying the outsize beast as though it were a massive bouquet of flowers, it may come through pride, leading one to believe that gallantry is most apparent when there is least to lose. By the time the chivalrous victim has actually grabbed the offending suitcase and discovered that it weighs over half a hundredweight, it has become unthinkable for this strong man to appear weaker than the not apparently very strong woman beside him. Particularly at stations like Milan Central and Cambridge, which have two of the longest platforms in Europe, the reward in the form of an averted rupture is well worth the ruse, even if, occasionally, the purple, pop-veined Galahad does finally put the suitcase down with a snide remark about transvestites and hor-mones.

The only luggage I ever really strain with is other people's, particularly old people's, no doubt because I see shades of myself, at some future date, still travelling and no longer with the charms to beguile anyone to come to my assistance. Again, at some future date, when the world has come to its senses, and ceased to destroy its forests and poison its seas, and the many bombs have all been dismantled, and the architects have got their come-uppance, and the railways of the world shall flourish and blossom and be clean and beautiful once more, I hope there will be a return of porters, with trolleys and flat rates and a lot of extremely helpful information.

Until such time, standards must be maintained as best they can by the loyal passengers of the ousted trains. It is, of course, harder to stand by a cause in decline, but religions and monarchs and emperors have bided their time until a just return was right, and so, too, must the illusory rulers of real glamour and style. I believe that, just as there have been times when books were banned and paintings burnt and ideas stifled – times which passed, as all times do – so shall the age of ugliness and convenience make its way out, while those who began and encouraged it crawl back under their stones. I see signs to prove this everywhere, like fleeting shadows of migratory birds, heralding the return of spring as they soar on their way.

These beliefs fall like dirty dishwater on to my daughter's newly washed hair. She is as deaf as a quarry-blaster to descriptions of railway delights. She tells me, cutting me to the quick, that she finds nothing more monotonous than crossing Europe by rail. I try to interpret her more wounding statements as the product of a passing fad, like skate-boarding or Cindy dolls, something that a girl can grow out of. 'Think of it as a vegetable,' I say, 'that you try many times, and eventually learn to like.' She offers to eat buckets of celery, garlic or even spinach, if she can only fly and meet me at our destination.

I try to coax her, my heretic daughter, with memories of some of the better journeys we have made together, in Germany and Switzerland, France, Italy, Spain. She is unreasonably prejudiced against the train. 'Think of the lovely picnics we have had,' I say, but she will only remember her cousin being sick on her from an upper bunk. 'Think of the compartment parties we have had. Think of the disco-dancing that time at Milan when all the passengers on the platform were staring into our frenzied cabin as we danced on the seats.' She remembers, and adds how the guard kept coming into our cabin, only to find us damply sitting in our places and the music silenced. And how he kept returning, not realising that we had a boy on guard, and so played what amounted to musical chairs. 'Well,' I say, triumphantly, 'didn't you like dancing on the train?'

'Yes, but I prefer discothèques.'

She is unbudgeable. She doesn't want to travel with her dear mama; she wants to fly.

One day, she will buy her own tickets, and it seems it will be very soon. Meanwhile, it is I who buy them, and since I am not Italian, I do not feel I need to conform to their law of voting and out-voting on all things. In the wider issues of the world I am a democrat; in the microcosm of my mother-hood, and when it comes to trains, I am a despot. The conversations and the coaxing are merely so that Iseult may bear her sentence with less pain. There is no option: we are all going by train – I with the hamper and a flask of brandy and a briefcase full of giant-size Toblerones, she with her

Ionesco plays and her music, and my son, Alexander, ironically, with his Happy Families and his Snap cards.

It is at moments like these that I most notice the generation gap. In many ways our tastes concur; in others, they could not be more different. The traits of our generations, like star signs, are hard to avoid. I come from the Sugar Ration Generation, the post-war baby boom. Although I am, modesty apart, a little young for this, I just scrape in by having been born in 1953, a year notable not only for that, but also for the death of Dylan Thomas and the abolition of the sugar ration in England. Thus I grew up with a scrimp-and-save attitude coupled with a constant reminder that I was lucky to have it so good. The Welfare State had just begun, heralded by the grumblings of those who had borne their aches and pains without it. Our refrigerator was always full of little saucers of unidentifiable and deteriorating left-overs, lined up like laboratory samples behind the half-finished lasagne and the cheese. One did not necessarily have to eat these examples of thrift; only recognise how wasteful it would be to throw anything away while still in an edible condition. My mother herself found it hard to the point of being virtually impossible to throw any food away until it got up and walked out of the fridge on its own cushion of mould, while years of rationing had produced a reaction of near hysteria at the sight of an uneaten crust or an unfinished dish of sago pudding. Needless to say, I never eat my crusts, or eat my apples down to the core, or eat any but the very leanest meat, but being a dutiful daughter I always finish my puddings.

My children belong, on the other hand, to the Heinz and Gerber generation, to the tall, large, big-boned, healthy and hypochondriacal generation reared on patent baby foods and vitamins. Even in the Black Forest, where babies were once fed on a diet of sugar dipped in slivovitz, and so used to sidle into adulthood in a dwarfed and brain-damaged state, mothers have turned to the dietetically balanced jar and tin. Even the daughters and sons of Japan have grown tall, while in Italy and Spain and South America, where the average height would rarely if ever have shot forth an acceptable

176

candidate for the London police force, huge offspring take their tiny parents out for meals. My family used to look like giants to the rest of the world; now millions of people are five foot ten, or six foot, or six foot six, and it is no longer enough, when meeting strangers at stations, to say, 'I am tall.' The red carnation is back in vogue. Buttonholes are the order of the day.

This generation of likely contenders for one big American football team is reared not only on height-promoting food, but also on brain-washing soap. Iseult is a classic of her kind, an adolescent shaped by soap operas, whose dreams and realities have merged to form an artificial, impenetrable bubble of expectation. Pocket money is meaningless, the Bank of Naples and the World Monetary Fund could scarcely pay for the needs and requisites of her ilk. *Dallas* and *Dynasty* have shaped their minds into a total plasticity. They have grown to believe that they shall inherit the earth as shown on television, and to view anything less as a grave but transitory disappointment. This is the age when toddlers cry if their clothes do not carry designer labels, when Christmas is a nightmare, and birthdays too.

That my own particular daughter has a nature as sweet as the huge reach of her dreams is a stroke of luck for which I am truly grateful. One day, I know, she will spread her wings and elect for jets, perhaps because nothing else travels fast enough to keep up with her dreams. In the mean time, under cogent protest, she continues to shuttle with me from London to Levanto, now through Paris, now through Amsterdam, pacing the corridors as restlessly as one of the Marchesa Casati's leopards, waiting for the day, which she is sure will come soon, when the VIP lounge is filled with white roses for her and her peers.

15

Chicago – my kind of town

Every year since my return from Venezuela I have travelled to America, both to visit my father and to publicise my books. This usually entails a lecture tour, which panders to my appetite for perpetual motion. My headquarters on these visits is Chicago.

I love to go slumming in Chicago. It has such gorgeous slums. The El(evated train) passes over them, shuddering above the rampant Victoriana of their wide eaves and verandahs and the elaborately carved lintels and doors. In a city that hosts some of the finest jewels of twentieth-century architecture, even the slums excel. America has not sinned as Europe has against the eye and the heart when it comes to building. It has not suffered from the dropping of bombs or the shelling of towns or the Vernacular Revival or the intelligent inane, such as the followers of the Bauhaus and its successors. Perhaps, having only recently acquired an architectural heritage, it has not felt the adolescent urge to rebel against it.

The town councils of Britain have achieved what even Hitler could not; they have destroyed centuries of public and domestic building, bringing whole cities under the demolition ball. In the wake of the bulldozers, in the ugly functional blocks built over the rubble, society itself has begun to crack and crumble. Communities are scattered like brick dust to be resettled among strangers. The scientists who claim they (with serious financing) can teach dolphins to sing six national anthems and thus promote world peace, and the hucksters who sell Moon Shuttle tickets to market-goers in small South American towns, have all practised smaller cons, lesser frauds, than the architects and town-planners of the last four decades who, under the guise of improvement, have destroyed what there was, good and bad, and left in its place a concrete purgatory.

'An architect builds his reputation on other people's land.' It used to be an honourable profession. Now it is an international disease, and all of Europe is afflicted by the same ruthless vandalism. The Renaissance palaces remain, and the Roman viaducts, and tens of millions of humbler houses and cottages down the centuries, and whatever smaller places have escaped the pogrom of the New Wave have begun to be called bijoux residences and cost a lot of money, while the tower blocks of the sixties, the so-called 'solution' to twentieth-century housing, have already started to collapse under their own stresses and strains.

All this to say that Chicago, Illinois, has survived the homicidal concern of many earlier planners, and its beautiful, eccentric houses and gardens have remained intact. One can see from the crow's-nest of the El that there is much to be desired in their condition, but the spent cookers and rusty fridges and torn wings of cars on the steps and in the gardens, coupled with the peeling paintwork and squares of cardboard over broken glass and bits and pieces nailed in odd places by way of repair, show that, picturesque as it may be, it is none the less a slum, a run-down area where hardship and poverty and under-privilege are permanent non-paying guests. Difficulty is a transitory lodger who goes the rounds of his neighbours. But there are, at least, neighbours there, and they are known to each other.

In these times of so-called democracy and civil rights, I often wonder why even the primeval right of every cavedweller is now so often denied. Everyone needs a home, not just for shelter, but for comfort and rest, and beauty is one of the greatest comforts there is. No animal fouls its own nest, so if generations of disaffected children have grown up to denigrate and destroy where they live, surely it is sign enough that their immediate environment does not feel like a home. There is no pride of place or pride of possession. There is something inhuman about so much modern planning.

Ten years from now, the slums of Chicago will still be there, exhibiting their patchwork façades to the passengers of the city's commuter train, but they will have been made comfortable inside, and modernised and repaired, and where the upturned cars and cookers now grow into the garden soil, there will be flowers, just as the miners once grew flowers in their tiny cottage gardens. Just as anywhere in the world, where people are happy with their homes, the plants trail on balconies, even if they are only cuttings from wayside bushes planted in disused tins.

The city of Ankara was, until the thirties, a small Turco-Roman village. Atatürk ordered a new capital for his Europeanised Turkey to be built around it, not in the elevated ghetto style of the tower block with its inherent despair and isolation, but in the Concrete Classic style of modern Turkey. As the city grew, grey in its grey cloud of smog, a different city sunk its roots around the hemline of the Ankaran hill. For forty years, these were the slums, pastel blue and red and green slums with occasional flashes of turquoise and darker blues in a vast, insanitary, colourful shanty-town. Gradually, as the ghetto-dwellers made their money and improved their homes, adding terraces and plumbing and electricity, people from the stark flats began to drift down into the shanty, finding its disadvantages outweighed by its charm. Ankara grows, and the pastel quilt around its feet grows with it, and will soon become almost as respectable as its wide boulevards. The human spirit is hard to put down.

Where does it go, though, in the industrial wastelands of New Jersey? There is something chokingly dreary about the route from New York City to Princeton. It is a derelict world that one sees, from either bus, or train, or car. The train, at least, gives it a certain unreality: it could be a massive set for an abandoned film of Armageddon. It could be a grey desert experiment. There used to be an antiquated shuttle that operated between the two places, dragging one from the seedy, hectic, glamorous, dirty, buzzing city on the shore to the sedate and prosperous university town with its Ivy League attitudes and its ivy-clad Gothic halls so redolent of older Oxford colleges.

The journey was like the filling of a badly made sandwich. It had the dry taste of old peanut butter. It was ash spread between the rich rye of New York and the fine hand-sliced white bread of Princeton. The train used to go very slowly, stopping at places that had no stations before hiccuping its way along the track. As though in sympathy with the wasteland it travelled through, it, too, had closed down its light industry, reducing its heating system to a small notice in each compartment showing how to adjust it, turn it off or restart it. This sign was like the obsolete signs on the disused factories' backs. Passengers – a mere handful of loyal commuters shunting along its desolate route – came armed with thick jumpers and coats. Perhaps that is why it has now been replaced by other, more efficient, rolling stock, still passing through the land of the dead but going now at such an increased speed that the sight of the aftermath of the Depression, with its torn wire fences enclosing boarded-up factories, is, somehow, no longer as disturbing as it used to be.

While staying at Princeton, I went to New York City a couple of times to see friends. The new train, though clean and aired and running to all its advertised specifications, disappointed me. I had braced myself to be shocked by the dull monotony of the wasted factories and the factory waste, and to be hurtled past them left a definite chink in the voyeuristic nostalgia I wished to enjoy. I had made the journey many times as a teenager, going backwards and forwards between Princeton and the Big City, with all its horror and fascination for an English-bred child.

A Holmesian desire to investigate the real extent of the wasteland and a masochistic impulse to wallow in its dusty nothingness led me to venture into a realm I abhor: that of the omnibus. I do not have a vocabulary large enough to express all that I feel about trains, whereas I could write a haiku on what I feel for a bus. (An omnibus is/Like a huge metal sick bag/It is not for me.) This is, of course, the bitter and twisted opinion of a poor road-traveller. It may seem to be a biased and unreasonable remark, but it is one that, together with any breakfast, lunch or tea, springs to my lips whenever I have had the misfortune to travel on its elevated wheels. Thus, when I took a bus from Princeton to the Big Apple and travelled, I was doing so not for comfort, but in the spirit of genuine enquiry.

The desert was still there, the man-made and abandoned desert of factories and warehouses and rubbish tips. As the streamlined bus approached, glazed, bored-looking people gathered around the stops. I will not say that they showed much sign of life, but they embarked, unassisted by the robust driver, and then sat in a stunned silence for many minutes together. As the vehicle steered its way out of the grey expanse of that particular part of New Jersey, these passengers began to exchange unintelligible snippets of information, and for a further half-hour the interior of the bus resounded to their manic swapping of monosyllables. Before entering the metropolis, however, they disembarked *en masse*, giving the impression that the sight of anything more alive than the suburbs would damage their fragile ecology. Living in the shadow of the dead factories must be like living in the wake of a nuclear holocaust. Scarcely any other living thing could survive there. No wayside flowers grew in the chemical ruin of the soil. Far away, the occasional stunted tree defied the general pollution, but still made one think that if it were ever to bear fruit, its seeds would be of clinker. It is a vale of clinker in a country of corn.

It was an American dream to turn the bone-shaking, tooth-rattling, unsprung cart that moved as though by miracle along a track, drawn not by horse but by the massed hot air of its nostrils, into a place of comfort and elegance. Mr Pullman dreamed of carriages like rooms: dining rooms, writing rooms, bedrooms, sitting rooms, with every comfort and convenience of home or club. He was the first to see the train as not merely functional. What began in America crossed the Atlantic and hailed an age of grace for all and sundry. The great trains made their names, which were collective names given to the destinations that they rolled towards. The Orient Express, the Trans-Siberian Railway, the Shanghai Express were names to vie with, but every journey was cushioned or decorated with Mr Pullman's ideas and their heirs. Long before the days of railway riot, with its frenzied rushing from station to station, the railway romance was begun. Even the engines and the goods trains were beautifully designed, with endless details intended merely to please the eye. Most trains today seem like troop trains by comparison.

Could any of those Hollywood films of the forties and fifties be made on a new Intercity 125? Marlene Dietrich, and Marilyn Monroe, and a host of others, would look utterly out of place, off set or on, in the dreary interiors of most modern trains. The railway romance has gone into hibernation. Mr Pullman (who died a very wealthy man) must be poor Mr Pullman by now, turning in his grave (or crematorial urn). The reign of discomfort and unattractiveness is upon us. The railways are blighted and shorn. Everywhere, it is old stations for new, old standards for new.

The old social privileges have been decried, but what once pertained to the few has not been given to the many. Together with the fine designs of the royal saloons and the first-class carriages, the comfort and loveliness of the third has been swept away, and a new uniform has been introduced. There are still first-class carriages and first-class tickets, on every form of transport but the bus. Despite all this, this chosen uniform is drab. Progress has begun to shunt backwards. Even the jet-set have to elbow their way to their jets through, nine times out of ten, awesomely boring airports. There is no Grand Central station of the air. What a pity that when the Paris mob cried out for Liberty, Equality and Fraternity, it did not add Quality to the list.

Out of the long winter, through which the mass desire to travel has never been so strong, nor the means to do so as available, the international ostriches have begun to pull their chilled heads out of the grubby sand. A few sparks of elegance can be seen again along certain lines, though these are still as rare as fireflies on a summer's night. The Orient Express glides backwards and forwards to Venice once more as a luxury venture. Yet still the roll-call of ostriches is called, and the ministers of transport raise their heads, and none of them has been called Pullman or even Gresley. So grace and style are still denied to the masses.

Despite the occasional branch-lines of squalor in America, there is no doubt that its railways have benefited most wonderfully from the 'bigger and better' mentality indigenous to that country. The great stations of the United States are great indeed, and, often, awesome enough to have been built as imperial mausoleums. In New York City alone, Grand Central station and Pennsylvania are more like city states than terminals. The United Nations, on a plenary session, cannot boast as many races gathered under one roof as at the grand bazaar of Penn. Central. It would not surprise me to learn that there was a maternity ward at one end and a morgue at the other, with people living their entire lives in between, trapped in the seething turmoil.

Train journeys in the United States are serious under-takings. In Europe, a tired or drunken traveller can never travel further than the confines of one country, and that can never be further than the distance to an international frontier. Once there, frontier guards and Customs officials, and even drug-addict dogs, will wake even the staunchest sleeper out of their slumber. In South America, the sight of anyone enjoying an uninterrupted rest is so galling to the assembled company that a fellow passenger will always be elected to awaken the sleeper to enquire about the quality of their sleep. In the absence of an election, a dictatorship will occur. Further north, beyond the Mexican border, a solitary traveller can sleep from state to state, from day to night, from day to day, in the long womb of its controlled interior. It is the cradle that never stops rocking after the lullaby is over. It is the biggest sleeping tablet in the world, and no one need ever swallow the pill, for it swallows them.

Only from Mexico City, it seems, does a train still run like the old trains, in sumptuous luxury, sweetening the sour pill of the end of the train ferries from Dover to Dunkerque. Right up until October of 1980 the night train to Paris was carried intact in its blue and gold glory, and nights begun in London ended in Paris with nothing to disturb the comfort of the two-berth cabins but the muffled shunting of the engines hauling the darkened cars into the belly of the ferry, and the quilted shouts of the platform guards.

The night train from Mexico City to Guadalajara is the sole prerogative of any Mexican peasant with the right fare. It is not expensive, just wonderful, and it is there for anyone and everyone who needs or wishes to use it.

My father's choice of home, now that he has retired from his mercurial careers, is Tlaquepaque, near Guadalajara. The name awakes some strange echoes in Iseult, who left the sugar plantation in the Andes where she was born with her native Spanish locked away in some secure part of her brain, and then, on learning a smattering of French and German and a fluent ease of English, seemed to have forgotten where she put the key. All she remembered of her first language as the years passed by was a popular song:

> Guadalajara es un llano,
> México es una laguna.

'Guadalajara is a plain, Mexico is a lake.' Then it went on, 'Give me some cactus to eat, even if it pricks your hand.' It always seemed to me a strange song, and stranger still that it should have crossed into such a remote part of the Venezuelan Andes as to be taught to her by the estate children. The last verse, as I remember it, told how the tree where the peacock used to sleep had fallen down, so that now the peacock would be reduced to sleeping on the ground like all the other animals.

In the light of this ditty, I find the attractions of Tlaquepaque too irresistible to miss. It has squeezed its turquoise plumes in between Siena and Turkey. The thousand eyes of its tail feathers wink to me across the Atlantic. The circus is in training again, which is to say the old leather cases are being sorted and allotted ready for the night train to Guadalajara. It steams into my dreams with such regularity that I feel my new address must be care of its guard.

16

'Through life's road, so dim and dirty / I have dragged to three and thirty'

It is November 1987, and I have traced the meandering course of the River Elsa through the province of Siena, past the walled medieval towns of Casole d'Elsa and Colle Val d'Elsa. Colle has sprawled from its ancient palazzos on the hill to cobwebs of new flats and offices, all grown up and cloned over the bomb sites of the war. The shadows of Siena are unique. Even on rainy days, the sun shines under the clouds, gathering the surreal rounded contours of the multiple hills into fistfuls of varying greens and golds. The oakwoods that form the natural haunt of wild boar keep their russet wigs all winter. Ten years ago, a wild boar was a rarity much prized in this land of hunters. In Italy, not even the sparrows or the larks are safe. Ironically, it was the huntsmen themselves who introduced a new stock of wild boar from Hungary. The animals might easily have been English for the zeal with which they embraced their new Tuscan home. As a token of their appreciation for having been lifted from their native freezing woods, they consumed the Tuscan acorns in industrial quantities and began to breed freak litters. Where once a wild sow would whelp one or, at most, two young, she now has litters of twelve and fifteen, all set to become large, ferocious, routing beasts under the autumn colours of the winter woods.

The farmers all complained, the huntsmen were delighted, the restaurateurs served *cinghiale* twice a day, devising new sauces and resuscitating old ones with which to season the rich meat. The farmers continued to bewail their trampled corn and their stampeded fields. The herds of boar began to overrun people's gardens with the ferocity of the Magyars of old. The same huntsmen who used to stalk the boar for days on end were now reduced to shooting the marauding herds from their bathroom windows and their kitchen terraces. Like the rabbits in Australia, and the stinging nettles of rural England, the experiment seemed to have got out of hand. New laws were considered, villagers talked of bringing the army in, isolated houses had to be protected by palings like the stockades of barbarous times. The oaks continued to flourish and burnish the landscape with their tarnished golds, but the wild boar became tainted with swine fever, and the herds diminished. All through the summer months the sick animals go down to the rivers to die. So the River Arno and the River Elsa flowed over and around a different kind of delicacy: *cinghiale* and pondweed, *cinghiale* and twigs. There is a Tuscan harvest of bloated pigs. The serenity of the landscape belies its continual ravagement. Millenniums of invading armies have passed this way with worse weapons than tusks or fever. On summer nights, the fireflies in the fields still form their magic carpet, and by day the hills still recede into mists of blue.

I feel the loveliness of Tuscany work on my blood like a tonic. My energy level rises with the river waters. In Florence the paintings on the ground floor are being baled and moved in case of flood. Meanwhile, the painter and I dream of Venice, already flooded for ever with its pale green canals. From London to Venice, from there to Turkey, and, somewhere on the horizon, the railed peacocks of Guadalajara. The plants that I shift and graft continually, from one house to the next, from one balcony to the next, have found a new terrace looking out over the towers of San Gimignano. Should the blue mist clear, the morning glories next year will trail their azure banners in its sight.

Out of the impermanence of the ritual upheaval, I must have my instant garden. The grouped herbs and the trailing geraniums and the car-sick bougainvillaeas are coaxed and bribed. The broderie anglaise of April lilacs and the wispy honey-scented wisteria are as much a part of the retinue as my own family. They need a home more than their wayward gardener does. So I will plant the fruit of my profits in stone, not in England, but in Italy.

Prospective houses, monasteries, towers and keeps knock at the door with the weekly post. The unfathomable system of postal delivery swallows up and spews out its mail with an unpredictable appetite. I examine the photographs and details of Tuscan properties, in various stages of decay, with eyes glazed by the pastel shades of Venetian canals. I believe in a cycle of effort and chance. It is a form of superstition. I don't think I will find either my Tuscan pile or my Venetian jewel by looking for it, yet nor do I believe that its chance arrival can happen unless I make the initial effort.

Now the years of my life have been packed and labelled, I shall send them on to London by registered freight. They will be weighed at the luggage office here in Italy, and withdrawn through Customs at London, Victoria. A Customs official will ask me, as he always does, 'Is this your own personal property and was it packed by you?'

And I shall say, 'Yes,' which will be a white lie on a canvas primed with many others. For I do not own the railways I travel on, nor the smalltalk or the stories of the passengers thereon. I am not the sole possessor of romantic dreams; the very romance depends on their being shared by generations. The allure of travel is universal, the sense of adventure that quickens my blood is borrowed and gleaned.

If, every year, I set out to travel, it is not so much in the vein of new discovery, but to cure an inherent blindness in myself. A reriding of the same track is merely my own ecological balance. It keeps me a part of society, albeit a society populated by the restless and the indigent and the refugee. If, at the end of every year, I have merely 'rediscovered America', as they say in Venezuela, I can feel no disappointment in following in Columbus's wake. I think, perhaps, that my continually returning to Genoa is now an almost conscious homage to the phrase. He didn't fall off the edge of the earth, and nor do we. Nor, even, do the derelicts who cling to the railway stations. The world is not flat, not even in Norfolk, not even in the Fens where its apparent flatness tries to creep into the soul and possess it with damp and a dull coat of mould.

Through all the Indies and the Andes and the Alps and the Apennines, the old journey of life continues. My family is scattered like shot from a gun, like the larks who have grown wise to the huntsmen's annual scourge, regathering at their different terminals. My trunks of unanswered letters have become unclosable. I must go to London to rethrow my dice. Visas and passports are needed (and travel cards for Mexico). The painter has travelled on ahead, weighed down by catalogues and boxes. He will wait for me at Bristol Temple Meads at an appointed time, with a white orchid in his buttonhole. Orchids are the new order of the day, because Robbie always wears one. Despite my constant weaving of the railway routes, I have only a vague notion of the current itineraries towards the Channel. Iseult cannot travel through France for technical reasons. I have agreed to arrive in London by a certain time on the following day. It is an old appointment, and one that has outlived the loss of my diary in Florence the summer before. There are trains to Belgium and Amsterdam. I choose Amsterdam for sentimental reasons, and the shuttle begins at Levante, drifting slowly to Genova Principe where the drug addicts and the transvestites will be meeting, as is their wont, at the station café. As the train halts at Sestri Levante, we hang out of the window, in search of the ubiquitous Enrico, hoping that he will be, by chance, on our platform for the two minutes of our stop. Despite his erratic timetable of day and night shifts, he is there, and the departure continues, bearing its necessary seal.

Amsterdam is a night away. Alexander is preparing to sleep, rearranging the lower bunk, one of many that have lulled his short life. I have described the romance of its thin houses and its grid of canals to Iseult. She has never been to Amsterdam. The film industry is growing there; she has heard talk of its recent premières. Amsterdam is the placebo of this new trial by train. A morning of waterside cafés is scheduled into the plan. Plan 197 of the year.

The guard is a bored insomniac who talks well into the night, making coffee in his tiny cabin and plying us with it, laced with his own nostalgia. As the journey progresses, Amsterdam shifts continually further and further away. By some strange geographical alchemy, we breakfast and lunch in Germany. Plan 198 is summarily hauled into being, on learning that the sea-crossing will be twelve hours long. The Dutch guard, as he slowly nears his motherland, has shown definite signs of invention in his descriptions of the Netherlands, a country that I know well (so long as I am not required to place it accurately on a map). I hope that his twelve-hour crossing is also coloured by fantasy. He is keen to impress Iseult, who has confessed to a disinclination to return to England. Perhaps by distancing the two countries he hopes to find favour.

On arrival, his diagnosis, at least of time, is proved correct. The afternoon tea in London, so long programmed, will not occur, and the white orchid is in danger of fading long before I get to see it. Only Ostend, I am informed, can speed us on our way. Belgium is to be invaded yet again, passed through by hurried troops on their way elsewhere. There are twelve minutes until the only possible train, and then we must change, twice, leaving exactly fifteen minutes to catch the hydrofoil to Dover.

'You'll never do it,' the ticket lady tells me in the near perfect English which is the monopoly of the Dutch. 'It needs too much luck.'

But I was born lucky, and running after trains is my self-appointed mission.

'What about Amsterdam?' Iseult enquires, and I remember how wonderful it is, and lead them to the station mouth to show them the vista of cobbled squares and trams and thin grey houses.

'You see.'

Iseult smiles. She understands my heart, and knows that the trek to Roosendaal and Ostend is our only alternative. The grey mists of each leg of the journey hover over the looped lace curtains and live painted ferns of every window that we pass. We discuss 'the future' and play cards, holding all the trumps in our hands. The hydrofoil is leaving as we arrive. We leave with it, through a haze of crocodile tears mutually shed to effect our embarkation.

The taxi from Victoria drops us off like random packages of

Italian mail, the children to inner London, myself to Paddington. The driver is unbribable. With two minutes to spare, I catch the Riviera Express.

'Love, like fire, cannot survive without continual movement, and it ceases to live as soon as it ceases to hope or fear.' However many lives or chances a person has, I used up some of mine on that journey to Bristol. The Riviera Express is destined for Cornwall. Its two categories of passengers are composed almost entirely of theatre-goers and drunks. I am two hours away from the white orchid, two hours from Bristol Temple Meads. I feel too excited to read or sleep, so my mind sifts through the other travellers. Across the aisle from me, a small, fidgety Liverpudlian is determined to make friends with the elderly couple in front of him. At his nervous elbow, and falling virtually into his lap, a large, drunken man in evening dress is fast asleep. He was already fast asleep at Paddington, breathing heavily into his wing collar.

Having successfully achieved all the connections of my journey, I feel, suddenly, extremely vulnerable, as though my entire future depended on the passing whim of strangers. I feel that if I miss my tryst with Robbie, I will miss my life. Half-closing my eyes, I try to imagine the centre gangway as a narrow canal and the littered floor a grey water surface, but although I have the inclination, the ticket collector just does not have the build to pass muster as a gondolier. I am startled out of the last shreds of my dream by the officious tapping of his metal hammer on the table beside the drunken sleeper's ear. After a long routine that might, in other times, have been adapted into something for Ginger Rogers or Fred Astaire, the tapping ceases, and the elderly offender springs from his seat, falling over the Liverpudlian in his wrath.

'How dare you tap!' he explodes. 'How dare you!'

The ticket collector stands his ground, protected from personal attack by the small Liverpudlian beside him, who tries by turns, ignoring the twelve stone of aroused drunken ire that sprawls over him, and fidgeting under it while making pleading eyes. Strings of foul abuse follow the collector, all shouted through the gritted teeth of what might otherwise pass for a real English gentleman. Long after the cause of his anger has disappeared, the man is still shouting, bow tie askew. Finally, the crushed and gasping Liverpudlian ventures to suggest, 'That's enough now.'

It is the perfect tinder to the other's rage. With threats and shoves, the sat-upon Northerner is forced out of his seat and tipped, bodily, into the gangway. Whatever sewage has been tipped into the Venetian canals in the last decade cannot have fallen far short of the filth that is then tipped verbally on top of him. He remains, stunned by the force of this abuse, on the floor. His attacker proves to have an encyclopaedic knowledge of the English language, ranging alphabetically, through every blasphemy and obscenity known to me and many more that are not. Finally, exhausted, he staggers away, whereupon the small, insulted victim jumps to his feet and begins to lunge and punch at the empty spaces around him, proclaiming to all and sundry that he would have made mincemeat of the big man, had he stayed. He continues with these aerobics for some minutes, moving almost mechanically like a farcical boxer in a cartoon. Eventually, the ticket collector creeps back and restrains the unhappy passenger in the straitjacket of his arms.

Sometimes the lands that the tracks carve through are veiled by a grey curtain of factories and pollution, or, sometimes, a curtain pulled tightly across the set patterns of suburban life. The cuttings slice past the bathroom windows and back gardens. There are few façades for the train. Sometimes the lands that the tracks carve through are politely hilly and white-peppered with sheep. Sometimes the lands are more rugged and wooded, or barren, where the tracks have been blasted through solid rock.

Out of the artery of human emotion run the small veins of trains, spilling over the whole world. They are spilling over the quick frontiers of Europe, where the bottled countries cherish their essence through the levelling invasions of American television and rock and roll. And the tracks weave their way across America itself, and across its southern continent, where there are few windows and fewer curtains. And the tracks run stolidly behind the imaginary Iron

Curtain. They run through every landscape and season, flirting with the shifts in climate, and the osmosis of its human cargo, with the surface coquetry of a courtesan. The trains are unmoved and unmovable, except along the predestined routes.

Night had settled like a shroud over the West Country. England was down till the morning, with only a few late stragglers nodding their way home. The carriage echoed with the empty complaint of the Liverpudlian: 'Well, what do you think of that?'

This seemed to me the perfect summary for people and trains, for the metal shell encasing, at any given moment, every aspect of human emotion. The train is both the antidote to temporary insanity and a straitjacket in itself, and it is a moment of release for those already incarcerated by the stranglehold of themselves, and, mostly, it is a capsule of life held in suspension, a vehicle for thought and emotion and a vehicle in which ordinary people may move across the land.

'Well, what do you think of that?'

I crossed my arms over my chest and held myself steady for the sight of a white orchid, and, later, a real canal and my own black and gold gondola, and the Orient Express rumbling across the causeway from Santa Lucia to the mainland beyond the lagoon with myself getting older and older, but probably no wiser, fading with the upholstery of the seats into a manic old age.

A NOTE ON THE AUTHOR

Lisa St Aubin de Terán was born in London in 1953. She married when she was sixteen, and for seven years managed a sugar plantation in the Venezuelan Andes. Since 1981 she has moved between Norfolk, Scotland, Bristol, the Italian Riviera, Siena, London and Paris. Her five novels have been published in more than a dozen languages, together with her poetry and short stories. She now lives in Venice with the painter Robbie Duff-Scott and her two children.